THE ANCIENT WORLD

REVISED EDITION

Contributing Authors:

Ira Peck, Elise Bauman, William Johnson

Historical Consultant:

Alvin Bernstein, Ph.D.
Chairman, Strategy and Politics Department
Naval War College

SCHOLASTIC INC.

Other titles in this series:
Early Civilizations in Asia, Africa, and the Americas
The Age of Europe
The Modern World

Curriculum Consultants:

William Guardia
San Antonio Independent School System
San Antonio, Texas

Helen Richardson
Fulton County School System
Atlanta, Georgia

Edward Praxmarer
Chicago Public School System
Chicago, Illinois

Staff:

Editorial Director: Carolyn Jackson
Production Editor: Penny Parsekian
Assistant Editor: Elise Bauman
Art Direction and Design: Irmgard Lochner
Text Illustrator: George Ulrich
Photo Researcher: Roberta Guerette
Maps: Irmgard Lochner and Wilhelmina Reyinga

No part of this publication may be
reproduced in whole or in part, or stored
in a retrieval system, or transmitted
in any form or by any means, electronic,
mechanical, photocopying, recording,
or otherwise, without written permission
of the publisher. For information
regarding permission, write to Scholastic
Text Division, 730 Broadway,
New York, NY 10003.

ISBN 0-590-34735-7

Copyright 1976, 1986 by Scholastic Inc.
All rights reserved.
Published by Scholastic Inc.
12 11 10 9 8   1 2 3 4 5/9
Printed in the U.S.A.

CONTENTS

A fancy wooden box from Sumer. An engraved pillar from Babylon. A beetle-shaped jewel box from Egypt. A stately temple in Athens, Greece. A graceful wall carving from Rome. They are all works of art from ancient civilizations—objects made, used, and admired by people who lived thousands of years ago. In the photographs on the following pages you will see these and other artworks from the past. But what kind of people actually made them? What kind of people used and admired them? And what were these people's lives like? To start answering these questions, look at the artworks in the photographs carefully. One way to learn about people from the past—one way to learn about history—is to examine and think about their art.

MESOPOTAMIA: The dawn of civilization probably took place 11,000 years ago, when farming first developed. The first cities sprang up 5500 years later in Sumer. Clues to ancient life are found in its ruins. The panels (far left) from a wooden box show soldiers (top panel) and war prisoners (bottom panel) going to see the king (top panel, in a sheepskin skirt). Some early kings of Sumer were looked upon as gods and carved in stone (left). A later king, Hammurabi of Babylon (below), receives laws from the sun god (seated).

EGYPT: Treasures found in the tombs of Egyptian kings have dazzled archaeologists. Pharaoh Tutankhamen's tomb held: a depiction of the king and his wife (above), a beetle-shaped jewel (right), and other colorful objects.

THE NEAR EAST: Relief of glazed bricks depicts archers from the royal guard (left).
GREECE: The ancient Greeks valued human achievements. They built temples like the Parthenon (top) to honor their deities and told stories about heroes such as Achilles and Odysseus (bottom).

ROME: *For centuries Roman soldiers belonged to the strongest army in the world (above), defending an empire where wealthy people often spent their leisure hours reading (top right). The fancy dining room with a sunken fountain (right) was in the home of a small-town merchant.*

ROME'S FALL: Eventually, the Roman Empire grew soft. Common people expected entertainment (below, top panel), musicians accompany gladiators. A whipper (bottom panel) forces a fighter to unchain a bull and bear. One of the strongest rulers of the period was Constantine (left), the first emperor to let Christians worship freely (right). But barbarian tribes kept chipping off pieces of the Roman Empire. Their art is shown in jewels (lower right).

INTRODUCTION
TO THE ANCIENT WORLD

You come home one evening and quickly turn on your favorite mystery show. Unfortunately, you are late—only 10 minutes remain till the end. A famous detective is about to reveal who stole the precious gems from the pharaoh's tomb. Step by step, she analyzes the clues that led her to the solution. It is all very clear, provided you were tuned in at the beginning. Because you weren't, you are baffled.

In a way, history is like a mystery show. Unless you tune into it at the beginning, you can't appreciate what is happening in the world right now. For today's events are not isolated from the past. They stem from the past. Today, for example, we take for granted the freedoms guaranteed in the Bill of Rights. They become more meaningful if you realize that two centuries ago they were quite daring. They set an example for the rest of the world.

How do historians get their information about the past? It all depends on how far back in time they go. Writing developed about 5000 years ago. To describe events that took place since then, historians rely mainly on written records. Some of the most enduring records were carved into stone. Others were inscribed in soft clay that later was baked hard.

Ancient Egyptians learned to write on *papyrus*. This was paper made from a tall plant that grew along the Nile River.

To describe events that took place before writing was developed, historians must rely on other evidence. It may be a biblical town like Jericho in Palestine that was dug up early in this century by special scientists called *archaeologists*. Or it might be a picture painted on the wall of a cave many thousands of years ago. Human events that took place before the development of writing are known as *prehistory*. Those that have taken place since the development of writing are known as *history*. Thus, what we call history is no more than 5000 years old.

Measuring Time. A word about the dates used by historians: In the Western world, the years are counted from the birth of Jesus. The years before his birth are accompanied by the letters "B.C."—before Christ. The years after his birth are accompanied by the letters "A.D." They stand for "anno Domini," which in Latin means "in the year of our Lord." In B.C. time, the numbers get *lower* as we go forward. One hundred B.C. follows 200 B.C. Julius Caesar was born in 100 B.C. He died in 44 B.C.

Until about 10,000 years ago, human life was a desperate struggle to survive.

The earliest people wandered the land, hunting and gathering food. They often lived in makeshift huts like the one in this cave painting (right).

Each day was spent in a never-ending search for food. People made crude weapons to hunt and fish. At first these weapons were made of stone, but gradually people learned to mine and use bronze and then iron. They fought savage beasts and fellow humans who were almost as savage. They gathered wild cereal grains, roots, and berries and cooked them over fires. They made clothes from animal skins stitched with bone needles.

Family groups sought shelter in caves or in very simple huts made of stones and wood. Some shelters were just holes in the ground covered with animal skins. Human beings during most of prehistory were nomads (NO-madz), or wanderers. They wandered all over the land looking for food. When they exhausted the food supply in one place, they moved on to another.

Then about 8000 B.C., a great change came. People began to live in a way that we would call *civilized*. They set up organized villages, developed governments, and traded goods. All this was due to one great discovery.

What do you think it was?

PART
1

MESOPOTAMIA

The experts aren't sure where it happened first. But most think that the dawn of civilization occurred in the northern part of the land called Mesopotamia (mess-oh-po-TAY-me-uh). Today it is called Iraq (ih-RAHK). Around 8000 B.C., people there learned to grow food for themselves. They noticed that when wild cereal grains were scattered on the ground, the seeds reproduced themselves in abundance. They began to sow the seeds in areas near hunting grounds. In time, people who hunted also made a discovery. It was easier to tame many kinds of animals than to hunt them. They began to pen up various kinds of wild animals, feed them, and breed them. The young animals that resulted were less wild than their parents. Cattle, pigs, goats, and sheep were raised for their meat, milk, and wool. Horses and donkeys were harnessed for their muscle power.

These discoveries enabled people to settle down. From nomadic hunters and gatherers, they became farmers who lived in permanent villages. They could now produce more food than they needed. This made it possible for some villagers to become crafts workers, or *artisans* (ART-is-ins). It also permitted trade between villages in grain, pottery, and raw materials. Some villagers became merchants.

Early farm villages were built along the fertile shores of great rivers. Two of these rivers, the Tigris (TIE-griss) and the Euphrates (YOU-fray-teez), flowed through Mesopotamia. The name Mesopotamia was given to this region by ancient Greek historians. It means "the land between the rivers." Each spring, the Tigris and the Euphrates overflowed, spreading silt and mud on either side for miles. This enriched soil was good for growing food, but the floods had to be controlled. Otherwise people lost their homes and villages. In the southern part of Mesopotamia, an area called Sumer, villagers built dikes to keep the rivers from flooding. Then they built canals and ditches in the land between the rivers. This was called irrigation.

The Fertile Crescent. Soon it was possible to irrigate land and grow food in the entire area, which otherwise was hot and dry. Sumer was part of a well-watered region that extended in a great arch from the eastern shore of the Mediterranean Sea to the Persian Gulf (see map p. 23). Historians call this region the Fertile Crescent.

The job of building dikes and canals in Sumer could not be done by one village

Ancient objects often supply
information about the past.
Samples from Sumer include: a
game board made of shells (above),
a dagger and sheath from a
cemetery (right), and Sumerian
writing on a clay tablet. Page 18:
Sumerian statues used in religious
worship.

alone. Several villages had to join together to build them and keep them in good condition. As they expanded outward, they became city-states that were ruled by kings and priests.

The city-states flourished from about 3500 B.C. to 2000 B.C. They had names like Nippur, Kish, Lagash, and Ur. What was the importance of these city-states? They were among the very first centers of *civilization*. The word "civilization" describes an advanced society in which people have developed a system of writing and excel in the arts. They have built temples, monuments, and palaces. They have used science and technology to master their natural environment. They have government and laws to regulate human life.

All of these characteristics can be found in the city-states of Sumer. The Sumerians were the first people to develop a written language. Sometime around 3500 B.C., they began using a wedge-shaped instrument called a stylus to inscribe symbols on clay tablets. This is *cuneiform* (kyu-NEE-uh-form) writing.

Many thousands of these tablets have been dug up in Mesopotamia in recent times. They tell us much about the civilizations that once flourished there. If history is the written record of human events, it may be said that history begins at Sumer.

MAP EXERCISE

This map shows where two of the earliest farming civilizations began. Use it to answer the following questions:

1. Which sea is directly east of Egypt?
2. The Nile River flows north into which sea?
3. Sumer was located between which two rivers?

4. How far was Ur from Babylon? From Memphis?

THE CRADLE OF CIVILIZATION

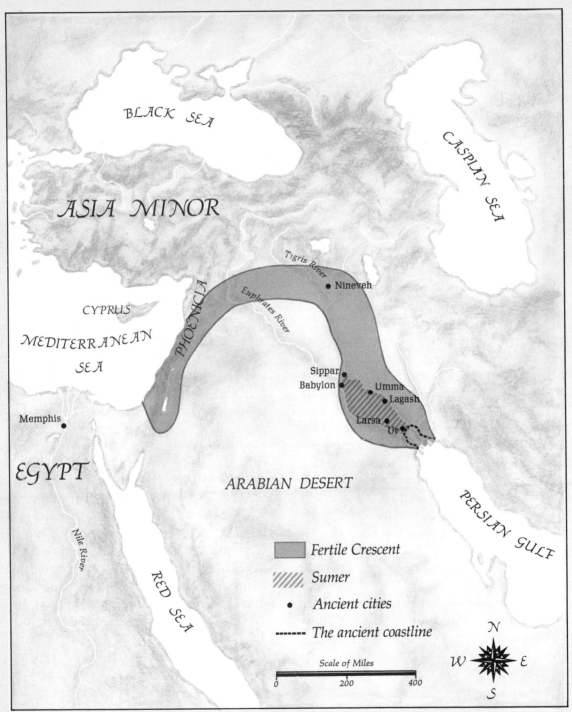

BLACK SEA

CASPIAN SEA

ASIA MINOR

Tigris River

Nineveh

CYPRUS

Euphrates River

PHOENICIA

MEDITERRANEAN
SEA

Sippar
Babylon

Umma
Lagash

Memphis

Larsa
Ur

EGYPT

ARABIAN DESERT

PERSIAN GULF

Nile River

RED SEA

Fertile Crescent

Sumer

Ancient cities

The ancient coastline

Scale of Miles

0   200   400

N
W   E
S

1
The Secret of the Desert

The land is a desert now. It is hot, dry, and barren. Only a few poor shepherds live on it. Yet once this land had great cities, and the fields were green with barley and wheat. Inside the cities were the palaces of powerful kings. There were beautiful temples to honor the gods. There were schools, workshops, and homes built of bricks. There were busy, crowded marketplaces.

These were the world's first cities. They were built more than 5,000 years ago in the land of Sumer.

The people of Sumer, called Sumerians (soo-MAYR-ee-uns), were first with many things. They invented the wagon wheel, the plow, and the sailboat. They baked clay and mud into bricks for build-ings. They melted metals such as copper and bronze, and shaped them in molds. They learned how to use numbers.

The greatest invention of the Sumerians was writing. Sumerians usually made their cuneiform inscriptions on a piece of wet clay. Thousands of pieces of clay with cuneiform writing have been dug up from the desert. They tell us much about the life, laws, and history of Sumer. So do the ruins of Sumerian cities like Ur (er). The cities have been dug up in the last 100 years by men and women who study how people lived long ago.

Finding Ur. In 1927, an Englishman named Sir Leonard Woolley dug down into the desert sand in southern Iraq. Woolley believed that the great city of Ur

At right, scientists explore the ancient burial ground at the city of Ur, where about 2000 common people and 16 kings were buried.

24

had once stood on this spot. Its ruins were probably buried beneath a mound of sand.

Woolley guessed that he was probably digging in a burial ground of Ur. He was right. Aided by Arab workers, he found about 2,000 graves. Nearly all were the graves of common people. The bodies were buried in the same way. Each was lying on its side, as if sleeping. Inside the coffins were beads, earrings, knives, and pins. Outside the coffins were jars of food and water, daggers, tools, mirrors, and combs. These were the things the dead would need for their trip to the next world.

Woolley also found 16 very large tombs in which kings were buried. They were built of stone or brick and had one or more rooms. When Woolley entered these tombs, he could hardly believe his eyes. The tombs were like underground palaces. He found not only the bones of kings, but the bones of the many people who had served them. These people had died with their kings, because they believed the kings were gods. The servants had entered their kings' tombs alive and then swallowed a drug that made death painless. They expected that they would then be able to serve their god-kings in the next world.

One of the 16 kings' tombs was very rich. At the tomb's entrance Woolley found the bodies of six guards in two neat rows. They had copper spears and helmets. Just inside the tomb were two wagons. Each was "pulled" by three oxen. The drivers were in the wagons. The leather reins were decorated with beads of silver and rich blue stones.

The bodies of nine women were leaning against one wall of the room. They were women of the king's court. All wore head coverings of rich beads, gold leaves, and silver combs.

The king himself was buried in a smaller room with men servants. The passage leading to the door of the king's room was lined with the skeletons of soldiers. All had daggers. One had a bundle of four spears with gold heads. Two others had sets of silver spears. Robbers had broken into the king's room and stolen most of its ornaments.

The royal tombs found by Woolley in Ur were extremely old. They were built between 2700 B.C. and 2500 B.C. What did these tombs tell Woolley about the people of Sumer at this time?

▪ They were very skilled people — builders, artisans, and artists.

▪ Their kings were treated as gods and had great power and wealth.

▪ Their merchants traded with many lands. Sumer had no metals or stones,

Sumerian kings, thought to be all powerful, are shown larger than life.

and very little wood. The metals, stones, and wood found in the tombs must have come from trade.

▪ Their soldiers had good weapons and were well trained.

▪ They knew how to write.

▪ They were ahead of all other peoples of their time.

✎ Quick Check

1. *How long ago were the cities of Sumer built? What kind of buildings did they have?*

2. *List at least three things first invented by the Sumerians. Which was most important?*

3. *When did modern people first learn about Sumer? What did Sir Leonard Woolley discover?*

4. *What do Sumerian tombs tell us about the people's religious beliefs? About their skills? About their dealings with other peoples?*

2
Daily Life in Sumer

"Look now at everything on earth,"
Rejoiced Ninurta, king of the land. "The
fields produce abundant grain. They
make happy the spirit of the gods."

This poem is part of a Sumerian "farmers' almanac" which served as a guide to successful farming. The land was very important to the people of Sumer. It was the source of most of the nation's wealth. In a bad year, a drought or a flood could bring famine.

Herding was as important as growing grain. Shepherds were responsible for the wool, milk, and cheese that almost everyone used. They too were affected by drought or flood.

The Sumerians prayed to many gods and goddesses, or *deities* (DEE-ih-teez), to ensure a good harvest and healthy animals. As shown in the poem, they believed that the gods and goddesses took a personal interest in the food supply. According to a myth, Inanna, goddess of love, could not decide whether to marry a farmer or a shepherd. She finally decided on the shepherd, perhaps because she liked cream. The farmer was luckier, though, because Inanna had a sharp tongue and a temper to match.

Some people in Sumer had little to do with the land. They lived in cities and worked at other jobs, such as making pottery. Because people lived close together, they needed laws and government.

How did the Sumerians govern themselves? They divided the land into different city-states. Unfortunately, this kind of organization did not, in the end, create a unified nation. The city-states of Sumer were seldom at peace. They fought each other almost constantly. They fought over property rights, water rights, or to gain control over another city-state.

God-Kings. In times of war, a Sumerian city chose a king to lead it. When the war was over, the king was supposed to give back his power. After a while, though, the kings kept their power and handed it down to their sons. They called themselves gods, and eventually the Sumerians believed that they were gods.

Once in a while, a great king would defeat the other city-states and set up a small empire. But these empires did not last long. One or more city-states would overthrow them. Then the city-states would start fighting again.

The people of Sumer were divided into three classes, or groups of people. The kings, nobles, priests, and rich landowners made up the highest class. The next class included farmers, tradespeople, soldiers, and artisans. Slaves made up the lowest class.

Slaves were sometimes bought and sold for their entire lifetimes, or they could be hired for a certain period of time. Although masters owned their slaves, no one considered slaves less than human. Anyone could become a slave by having bad luck or by being captured in a war. Slaves had some rights. They could own property and trade goods. They could even save money to buy their freedom.

In a Sumerian family, men were the heads of the households. They could own property and trade goods. They arranged their daughters' marriages and their sons' educations. If a man had debts, he was allowed to hire or sell his wife and children as slaves.

However, women had some power, too. When a woman married, her father usually gave a dowry, which was a gift of money or goods. A wife was permitted to use her dowry as she pleased. Sometimes she would use it to start her own business. Women in Sumer could be merchants, tavern owners, and landowners.

From what has been found in the ruins of Sumer, we can piece together some facts about life there. The rest can only be imagined. Suppose, for instance, that we are in a busy market street in the city of Lagash. Booths with all kinds of goods for sale line the mud-brick buildings. Cloth awnings cover the booths to shade them from the hot sun.

Two Sumerian women, Ninti and Shubad, are walking down the street. Ninti is a weaver who weaves linen from flax. Shubad and her husband are farmers who grow flax and millet, a kind of grain. Both women wear simple, linen tunics that reach to their knees. Because they are not slaves, each wears a thin veil draped about her face. Ninti is wealthy, so she also wears rings and bracelets.

SHUBAD: How is business lately, Ninti? That cloth that you have been making looks very fine.

NINTI: Oh, business couldn't be better.

The soldiers who have been fighting in the war against Umma tear their clothes to shreds all the time. They buy a lot of cloth from me. The only problem is that the flax I use to weave linen costs too much.

SHUBAD: Yes, our crops were short this year because of the floods. That's why the price is so high. But the new crop will be ready in two weeks.

NINTI: Business aside, how are your children, Shubad?

31

This figure was probably a Sumerian offering to the deities.

SHUBAD: Oh, they're fine. But I'm worried about my oldest son, Dumuzi. His father says that we have so many debts to pay that he might have to hire Dumuzi out as a slave for a few years.

NINTI: Dumuzi is too young to leave home, Shubad. Maybe I could help you out.

SHUBAD: How?

NINTI: Well, you know my cousin, Shara?

She's a very good weaver and has decided to go into business for herself. She will be needing a lot of flax to work with, and she wants to be assured of a good supply. I think she would buy all the flax that you and your husband grow.

SHUBAD: This is just what we need, the assurance that we can sell everything we grow. My entire dowry was used to buy the flax field, and I sometimes wonder if I made the right decision. We have nothing to spare. Is it possible that your cousin would pay in advance?

NINTI: Flax has been in short supply lately, and I know she's anxious to secure enough to get her company started. I'll ask her right away.

✎ Quick Check

1. *What were some of the ways that Sumerians made a living?*

2. *Would you describe Sumer as a unified nation? Why, or why not? How did the need for a ruler or king arise? How did these rulers keep their power and pass it on?*

3. *What kind of religion did Sumer have? What did most of their prayers concern?*

4. *How many classes were there in Sumerian society? In what class were soldiers? Priests? Farmers? Rich landowners? Kings?*

5. *How might a person become a slave? What rights did slaves have? How was it possible to get out of slavery?*

6. *What was the role of the husband in the Sumerian family? What powers did women have?*

3
The Fall of the Kingdom

What finally happened to the cities of Sumer? Sumer was a flat land, open to attack from almost every side. All around it were rough tribesmen, mainly poor shepherds. These outsiders were jealous of the rich cities and fields of the Sumerians. They often attacked the Sumerian cities. Usually the Sumerians were able to defeat them. But by about 2200 B.C., the Sumerian cities had become weak from constant fighting. Their enemies had become stronger. Soon the enemies began to take over the cities of Sumer. Here is the story about the fall of the last great city, Ur. It happened in 2000 B.C.

King Ibbi-Sin of Ur was in great trouble. Desert tribesmen were outside the walls of his city. They were getting ready to attack it. The brick wall around Ur was thick and strong. But the supply of food in the city was getting low. Food prices had gone way up. Fish and barley were selling at 50 times the usual price. Many people were starving. How long could the city hold out?

King Ibbi-Sin had written to his governors and begged for help. He needed both food and soldiers. But the governors took advantage of his weakness. Many refused to obey him any longer. One governor made a deal with Ibbi-Sin. He would send help if Ibbi-Sin would make him king of two cities. Ibbi-Sin agreed and made him king. But no help came. Instead, the new king began to take over other cities.

At last the tribesmen broke into Ur and took Ibbi-Sin away as a prisoner. Then they destroyed the great city and its temple. A poet of Sumer wrote a lament, a sad poem, about the fall of Ur. This is part of it:

The walls of Ur were broken: The people
  mourn...
At the tall gates, where people liked to
  walk, dead bodies lay about.
In its wide streets, where feasts were held,
  scattered they lay...
Corpses, like fat placed in the sun, melted
  away....
The old men and women who could not
  leave their houses were overcome by
  fire.
The babies lying in their mothers' laps
  were carried off....
Our way of life perished. The people
  mourn.

✎ **Quick Check**

1. *Why was Sumer open to attack? Who wanted to attack it, and why?*

2. *What was the last great Sumerian city to fall? When did this happen?*

3. *Why did King Ibbi-Sin need help? What kind of deal did he make to save his city? Did it work? Explain.*

4
Hammurabi's Code

The fall of Ur marked the end of the Sumerians as a people. The cities of Sumer were taken over by the neighboring tribes. These invaders soon became city people themselves. They copied the ways of the Sumerians, especially their religion and arts. They made the city of Babylon (BAB-uh-lon) their capital. They built a new civilization called Babylonia (bab-uh-LO-nee-uh). One of the greatest kings of Babylon was Hammurabi (HAM-uh-RAHB-ee). His famous code was one of the first sets of laws used to rule a kingdom.

In the following dialogue you can see how this code might have been applied.

The scene: a courtroom in the city of Babylon, capital of the kingdom of Babylonia.

The action: the owner of a private house is suing the man who built it.

The year: about 1700 B.C.

JUDGE: Who is the accuser in this case?

TURIBUM: It is I, Turibum, a pottery maker who resides in this city.

JUDGE: And who is the accused?

LUKANI: It is I, Lukani, a builder who also resides in this city.

JUDGE: Very well, then, Turibum, what is your complaint?

TURIBUM: Your honor, I bought my home from Lukani, the builder, less than a year ago. Within a few weeks, large cracks began to appear in the walls. I told Lukani that the house was unsafe and that he had to repair it. He kept promising me that he would, but he never did. Then, three weeks ago, the roof caved in. The house and all of my furniture were destroyed.

JUDGE: Was anyone in the house hurt?

TURIBUM: Fortunately, your honor, my wife and I were not at home that day. But our slave was, and she received severe injuries. I doubt whether she shall ever be able to work again.

JUDGE: Those are very serious charges, Turibum. Well, Lukani, what do you have to say in your defense?

LUKANI: Your honor, I am an honest man, I swear it. I really intended to repair Turibum's house, but I was so busy. There just wasn't enough time...

JUDGE: That's a very poor excuse, Lukani. The laws of our king, Hammurabi, make you responsible for the safety of the houses you build. Therefore I order you to rebuild the house and replace the furniture at your own expense. I also order you to pay the medical expenses of the injured slave. If she cannot work again, you must replace her or pay Turibum the amount needed to replace her. This case is closed. Next case!

Early Justice. The laws of King Hammurabi of Babylonia (about 1728-1686 B.C.) are among the oldest on record. They were engraved on a stone pillar that once stood in the temple of the god Marduk in Babylon. The stone was dug up early in this century, and its 282 laws became known as Hammurabi's Code. The code tells us a great deal about life in ancient Babylonia. Some of the laws seem quite humane. If a farmer's crops were ruined by a drought, for example, he did not have to pay his creditors that year.

Other laws seem very primitive. A man's wife and children were considered his property. To pay his debts, he could sell them into slavery for up to three years.

There were different standards of justice for noblemen, freemen (commoners), and slaves. If a freeman struck a nobleman, for example, he would be whipped in public as an example to others. But if he struck a member of his own class, he would only have to pay a fine of sixty *shekels* (half-ounce silver coins). If the victim was a slave, he would have to pay a fine equal to half the slave's value.

Some punishments were based on the ancient law of "an eye for an eye." A man who assaulted another and put out his eye would have his own eye put out. If he broke a bone, his own bone would be broken. The punishment for a son who struck his father was even more severe. His hand would be cut off. Yet Hammurabi's Code also contained some provisions that seem very advanced. For example, if a man was robbed and the robber was not caught, the victim received payment from the local government.

Now let us take a closer look at the stone pillar containing Hammurabi's Code. At the top is a picture carved into the stone. It shows Hammurabi receiving his code of laws from the sun god, Shamash, who is also the god of justice. Hammurabi says that the gods called on him "to make justice visible in the land." His goal is "to destroy the wicked person and the evil-doer, so that the strong may

Hammurabi (standing) had his code inscribed on a stone pillar. The laws governed many problems humans still face today.

not injure the weak." Below this introduction are Hammurabi's laws. They are arranged in an orderly form and deal with a wide range of subjects. Among them are the family, offenses against property, and business regulations. Some of these laws show that Hammurabi was concerned with the same problems that we have today. Our society, however, would not tolerate the cruel punishments that were common in his time. Here are just a few of Hammurabi's laws.

▪ If a man's wife squanders his money and makes him poor, he may divorce her.

He will not have to give her divorce money.

▪ If a man accuses another of murder and cannot prove it, the accuser shall be put to death.

▪ If a surgeon operates on a freeman and causes him to die, the surgeon's hand shall be cut off.

▪ If a farmer opens his ditch for irrigation and carelessly floods his neighbor's fields, he shall have to pay for the crops he has ruined.

▪ If a tavernkeeper adds water to his beer to increase his profits, he shall be drowned in a river.

At the end of the code, Hammurabi advises his successors to uphold his laws. Those who do will be blessed. But a king who changes his words will suffer a terrible fate. "May the mighty gods of heaven and earth curse him," Hammurabi says. "May his land, his warriors, his people, and his nation be cursed."

✎ Quick Check

1. *On what civilization was Babylonian civilization built? What parts of the older civilization did it copy?*

2. *Why was Hammurabi remembered as a leader? When did he rule?*

3. *Give an example of a law based on the "eye for an eye" principle. Give an example of a law that seems more advanced. Give an example of a punishment that seems harsh today.*

4. *Do Babylonian laws seem to show that problems have changed over the centuries, or remained very much the same? Explain.*

5
The Assyrians, Brutal Conquerors

Nineveh is laid waste; who will bemoan her?"

The Hebrew prophet Nahum made this prediction about the capital of the Assyrian Empire. In 612 B.C., his prediction came true. The city was attacked by three armies, the Scythians, the Chaldeans, and the Medes. They sacked and burned Nineveh. No one felt sorry for the Assyrians. They were a violent people who thrived on war, and other nations despised them.

Away from the battlefield, however, the Assyrians built a rich and varied civilization in northeastern Mesopotamia. Nineveh was a wealthy and beautiful city. It was built to withstand invaders. The outer stone wall was 200 feet high, and three chariots could ride abreast on top of it. Inside this wall, a maze of moats and inner walls protected over 30 temples. They gleamed with ornaments of gold and silver. Splendid palaces were surrounded with lush gardens scented by fruit trees and flowers. Canals carried water to the city from the nearby Tigris River. There was enough water for all the 175,000 people of Nineveh.

King's Pleasures. The Assyrians liked to live well. Their last king, Ashurbanipal (ah-sur-BAHN-ih-pahl) loved eating, drinking, and entertaining. He gave many lavish feasts. His guests were entertained by musicians who played harps, flutes, and other instruments.

In the daytime Ashurbanipal liked to hunt. Earlier kings had hunted for food, but Ashurbanipal hunted for fun. He hunted wild bulls, donkeys, and goats, but his favorite prey was the lion. He

Gifts such as horses were often given to appease Assyrian kings (above). Page 41: A stone carving from Nineveh shows a horseman hunting lions (top) and King Ashurbanipal pouring wine over the dead animals.

brought in African lions and kept them in huge parks. During a hunt, servants would drive a lion down a path, and Ashurbanipal would chase after it in a chariot. Lions were sometimes hunted on foot, which was far more dangerous. After a lion was killed, the king would always pour precious oils over the body to satisfy any angry spirits.

The king was fond of art. The walls of Nineveh were decorated with many carvings that showed battles, legends, and daily life in Assyria. Huge sculptures of winged people and animals adorned gardens and courtyards. Some survived to modern times.

However, the best surviving record of Assyria is Ashurbanipal's library. As far as we know, it is the first library ever built. When it was discovered in the 19th century, it had more than 22,000 clay tablets written in Sumerian-style cuneiform.

What was written on those tablets? They were mostly records of war and heroes and stories of the Assyrian gods. Here is a story of the gods that was part of the library. It is called, "The Reason that the Seasons Change."

When the world began, the seasons did not change. It was always springtime.

One day the goddess Ishtar (ISH-tar) discovered that her lover, Tammuz (TAH-mooz), had descended to the underworld to live with Allatu (ahl-LAH-too), queen of the underworld. Ishtar decided to go to the underworld to bring Tammuz back. To see the queen, she had to pass through a series of seven gates. At each gate, Ishtar was forced to remove some part of her clothing. First she took off her crown, then her jewelry, then her gown. Naked, she was allowed to see Allatu. Ishtar was furious at her humiliation. She attacked Allatu. The queen became angry and cursed Ishtar with many diseases.

While Ishtar suffered in the underworld, it was winter. The leaves fell, and the crops withered. Finally the god Ea (EE-uh) decided to save Ishtar. He sent a messenger to the queen. The messenger forced Allatu to pour holy water on Ishtar, thereby curing her. Ishtar was led out through the seven gates and got her crown, clothes, and ornaments back. After leaving the underworld, she was happy and spring came again. Tammuz came back to live with her for six months. Then he went back to the underworld again, and it was winter. This cycle repeats itself every year.

This legend provided the Assyrians with a romantic explanation for a natural

Ashurbanipal liked to live well. This stone carving shows the king (reclining) and his wife (sitting) feasting in a royal arbor at Nineveh.

occurrence. For us, it is a good example of the cruelty of the Assyrian gods. They responded to trouble with aggression, just like the Assyrians.

Cruel Conquerors. The Assyrians survived by learning to fight better than other people. They built a great empire on the wealth of captured cities. They also taxed the people they conquered. However, sometimes the Assyrians were so destructive there wasn't anyone left to tax.

When the Assyrians attacked a city, they gave the people a choice. They could either surrender or fight. Few could match the training, iron weapons, horses, and siege equipment of the Assyrians. If a city was captured, its people were treated mercilessly. Sometimes they were forced to become slaves. Other times they were murdered. The Assyrians also prided themselves on destroying the temples, tombs, and holy places of their enemies. Ashurbanipal recorded the destruction of the city of Elam in 640 B.C.

I have destroyed the temple of Susa, which was built of enamelled brick…I have utterly laid waste the sanctuaries of Elam. I have scattered their divinites to the four winds. My soldiers entered their sacred groves, which no stranger ever entered. They laid bare their mysteries and burned them.

The Assyrians conquered many nations. At the height of their empire, which lasted more than 500 years (1116 B.C.-605 B.C.), they controlled Egypt and most of the countries of the Fertile Crescent. Then, abruptly, their power and glory came to an end, and they were succeeded by a Babylonian people called the Chaldeans. They had ruled an empire on strength, but they were no match for the combined strengths of other nations.

✎ Quick Check

1. When did the Assyrian Empire flourish? Why was it hated by other nations?

2. What was the capital of Assyria? Describe it.

3. Who was Ashurbanipal? What types of things did he do for entertainment? What did he establish that was the first of its kind?

4. Describe the Assyrian war machine. How did the Assyrians treat the people they defeated?

MAP EXERCISE

By 625 B.C., Assyria ruled over much of the Near East. Use this map to answer the following questions:

1. On what river was Nineveh located? Name one other city within the Assyrian Empire.

2. What three bodies of water bordered on the Assyrian Empire? Into what body of water did the Tigris and Euphrates empty?

3. Name two ancient lands that were at least partly under Assyria's influence in 625 B.C.

THE ASSYRIAN EMPIRE

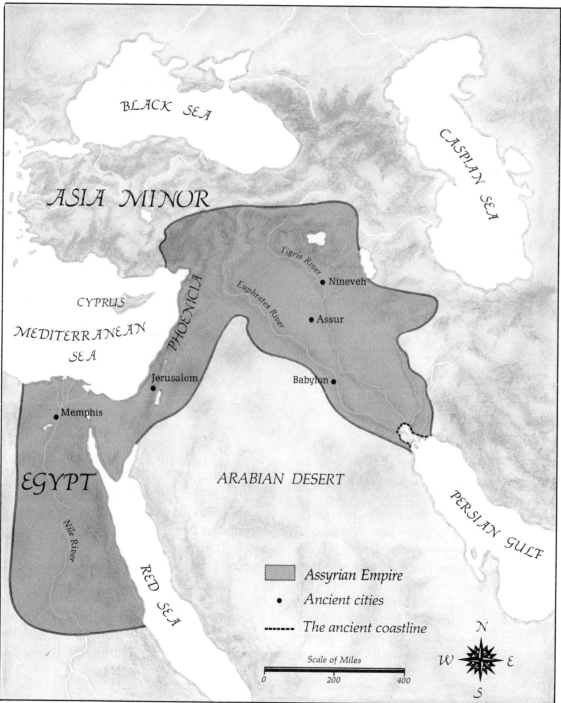

BLACK SEA

CASPIAN SEA

ASIA MINOR

CYPRUS

MEDITERRANEAN
SEA

PHOENICIA

Tigris River

Euphrates River

• Nineveh

• Assur

• Jerusalem

Babylon •

• Memphis

EGYPT

Nile River

ARABIAN DESERT

RED SEA

PERSIAN GULF

Assyrian Empire

• Ancient cities

------- The ancient coastline

Scale of Miles

0   200   400

N
W   E
S

PART 1

Review and Skills Exercises

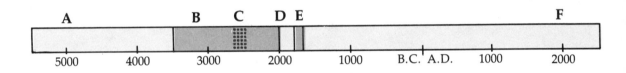

A   B   C   D E   F

5000   4000   3000   2000   1000   B.C.   A.D.   1000   2000

Putting Events in Order

Chapters 1-5 described the earliest civilizations and some of the ways that we have learned about those civilizations. Here is a time line with letters placed on the approximate dates when certain important events took place. Below is a list of events that took place during the time period shown on the time line. The events are not in order. Decide which event belongs with each letter, A-F. Write the letters on a sheet of paper. By each letter write the description of the proper event.

- King Hammurabi of Babylonia lives.
- Ur falls.
- Sixteen royal tombs of Ur are built.
- Sir Leonard Woolley discovers 16 royal tombs of Ur.
- First writing developed.
- First cities in Sumer are built.

Bonus: Interpreting Events. Choose one of the events from the time line. Write a brief explanation of the importance of the event.

Drawing Conclusions

Drawing conclusions involves looking carefully at information and making a judgment based on that information. Refer to the information in Chapter 5 on Hammurabi's Code. Use the information to draw conclusions about Babylonian society and answer the following questions.

1. Based on what you have read, do you think farmers were an important part of Babylonian society? Explain.

2. How did Hammurabi's Code protect consumers (people who buy goods or services)?

3. How was the method in which Hammurabi's Code came into existence different from the way we make laws in the United States today? What does this tell you about Babylonian beliefs?

4. What attitudes did Babylonian society have toward women?

5. Based on the laws, how do we know that there were different classes in Babylonian society?

6. One of the laws sets capital punishment as the penalty if a person accused another of murder and could not prove it. Why do you think this was such a serious offense?

Building Vocabulary

On a sheet of paper, write the numbers 1-12. The numbers correspond to the numbered blanks in the paragraph below. Beside each number write the word from the list that best fits in each space. You will not need all the words in the list.

advanced	engraved
apprentices	evolved
artisans	invaders
boundary	irrigated
citizens	painted
cuneiform	provisions
empires	standards

We have learned much about ancient Sumer from samples of ____1____ writing found at excavation sites. In addition, we have gained insight into this ____2____ civilization, which ____3____ from small farming villages into large cities, from many items unearthed at royal tombs. We know, for example, that the Sumerians ____4____ their crops and had a number of skilled artists and ____5____, or craftspeople. Sumer was not a peaceful place. From time to time, kings took over cities and created ____6____. ____7____ of one city would quarrel with those of another over ____8____ lines. Sumer was eventually overcome by ____9____ who established a civilization called Babylonia.

We have learned about a Babylonian system of justice from a pillar ____10____ with a set of laws. The laws, known now as Hammurabi's Code, set different ____11____ of justice for people. The code also contained measures, or ____12____, for dealing with crimes.

PART
2
EGYPT

I t has wonders more than any other land. It has works so great that they cannot be described."

A Greek writer of history named Herodotus (heh-ROD-uh-tus) said this about Egypt in the fifth century B.C. He had seen many great wonders in his time. But nothing he saw compared with Egypt's great pyramids. The pyramids were already 2,000 years old when Herodotus saw them. They are still standing today, 2,500 years later.

Why was Egypt able to make such great buildings so long ago? Egypt was a very fortunate land. It had the Nile River. This river starts in central Africa and flows 4,000 miles north to the Mediterranean Sea. Most of Egypt was a hot, dry desert where nothing would grow. But late every summer the Nile overflowed and flooded the land. It left a layer of rich mud that was good for growing food. That was the "gift of the Nile."

During the growing season, the sides of the Nile were green with wheat and barley plants. This strip of fertile land was from eight to 13 miles wide. At the Mediterranean Sea, it fanned out to form a triangle 150 miles wide. This is called a *delta*. On it was grass for herds of cattle to eat. Papyrus grew in the marshes, and many birds made their homes there.

The Egyptians pounded papyrus to make the world's first paper. On it they wrote symbols to stand for ideas and sounds. This kind of writing is called *hieroglyphics*.

Almost all of Egypt's people lived on the land near the Nile. They were dependent upon the river for their very lives. If it overflowed too much, villages could be covered with water. If it overflowed too little, not much land could be planted and people went hungry. Because they needed the river so much, the people of Egypt learned to cooperate. Together, they built a great civilization.

The Egyptians began by digging large holes that filled with water when the river overflowed. Then they built dikes to hold the water back when there was too much. When more water was needed, the dikes could be opened. They built canals and ditches to carry this water to their fields. They also drained swamps to create more land for crops.

The villages had to join together to do this work. Gradually cities formed and governments were organized. Unlike Sumerian cities, Egyptian cities could often work together. Egypt became the first united nation in history.

About 3100 B.C., a king from the south of Egypt defeated the kingdom in the north and joined the two lands. This king, Menes (MEE-nees), was the first of Egypt's many pharaohs (FAIR-ohz), rulers who were believed to be gods. Under the rule of the pharaohs, Egypt became a great nation that lasted for 3000 years.

ANCIENT EGYPT

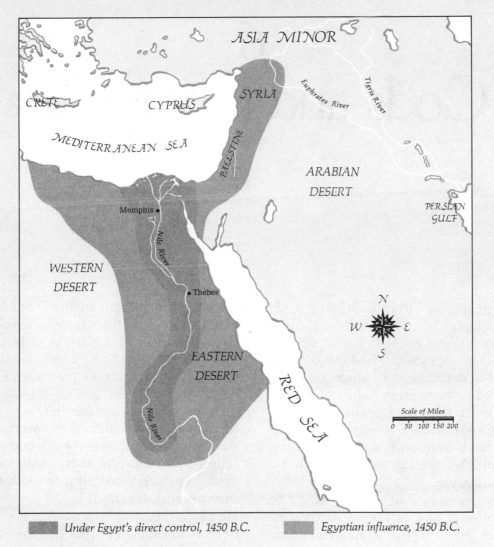

Under Egypt's direct control, 1450 B.C.   Egyptian influence, 1450 B.C.

MAP EXERCISE

By 1450 B.C., the influence of Egypt had spread beyond the Nile. Use this map to answer the following questions:

1. Egypt controlled the Nile River for how many miles south of the Mediterranean Sea?

2. How far was Memphis from Thebes?

3. What two other ancient lands were under Egypt's influence in 1450 B.C.?

51

6
Gods and Goddesses

The people of Egypt had many gods and goddesses who, they believed, ruled their lives. These gods often took strange forms. One, Bes (behs), had the body of a dwarf and the head of a lion. He was supposed to scare off evil spirits.

The most popular Egyptian god was Osiris (oh-SEER-iss). Wealthy Egyptians spent much time and money preparing for death. Yet the Egyptians were not a gloomy people. They believed strongly in life after death. This afterlife would be a happy one, just as life on earth was. And, according to the Egyptians, Osiris was the god who had made life after death possible.

The Egyptians believed that Osiris had once ruled Egypt as a king in human form. Osiris had taught them to plant food and made them civilized. But Osiris had a brother, Seth, who was jealous of him. Seth locked Osiris in a box and threw it into the Nile. Later he cut the body of Osiris into 14 pieces and scattered them.

Osiris had a sister, Isis (EYE-sis), who loved him. She searched the swamps of the Nile for the pieces of his body. She found them all, and then wept for her young brother. According to the legend, the sun god, Re (ray), heard her crying. He pitied Isis, and sent down a god from heaven to help her. This god, who had the head of a jackal, fitted the pieces of Osiris together. Then he and Isis wrapped the body in linen bandages and prayed for it. Osiris rose from the dead and became king in the next world.

For Egyptians, the god Osiris (left) was a symbol of life after death. Page 48: Another symbol Egyptians favored was a mythological creature, the sphinx. It represented royalty.

The Egyptians believed that they too could rise from the dead if their bodies were treated in the same way. This meant making mummies of their bodies.

Making Mummies. How was an Egyptian mummy made? First the dead body was treated with salts, spices, and resins to dry and shrink it. Then it was completely wrapped with layers of linen bandages to preserve it. The family of the dead person wept, and priests said prayers. Finally, the mummy was put inside a stone tomb. Food, clothes and furniture were also put inside the tomb. It was thought that the dead person would need these in the afterlife.

The mummies of Egyptian pharaohs and nobles were placed in elaborate coffins before burial (left).

Only wealthy Egyptians could afford to be buried in this way. But even poor Egyptians prepared themselves for life after death. They were usually wrapped in rough white cloth. Then they were buried in sand graves with scraps of food and tools.

The Tears of Isis. Osiris was thought to be the god who brought the dead back to life. The Egyptians believed that he gave a new life not only to people, but to the land as well. How did Osiris make the land come alive? During the summer, Egypt was so dry that nothing could grow in the soil. Even the sides of the Nile were bare. The land was dead.

Late in the summer the Nile would begin to rise and finally overflow. The Egyptians believed that the tears of Isis crying for Osiris made the river flood. By November the flood waters went back to the Nile. But now the sides of the river were wet with mud again. This was the time to plant food.

The story of Osiris gave the Egyptians hope. It gave them hope that each year food would grow again along the Nile. And it gave them hope of everlasting life after death.

✎ Quick Check

1. *Who was Egypt's most popular god? Why?*

2. *Who was Isis? What human emotions did she show?*

3. *What was the purpose of mummification? How was it done?*

4. *Describe the differences between the burial of a wealthy Egyptian and a poor one.*

7
Building the Pyramids

The pyramids of Egypt are one of the great wonders of the world. Most of the buildings of the ancient world have crumbled, but some of the mighty pyramids still stand. They line the western side of the Nile in northern Egypt. The pyramids are solid stone buildings. They have a square base and sides shaped like triangles that meet in a point at the top.

How were these enormous buildings built? Why were they built? For thousands of years after the fall of Egypt, people were not really sure. Now we know enough about the ancient Egyptians to answer these questions.

The year: about 2670 B.C.
The place: the west side of the Nile at Giza (GHEE-zuh).

The great blocks of stone weighed more than two tons each. Gangs of men strained to pull them up the high ramp. Egypt did not have horses or wheels yet. The stones were tied on flat wooden sleds and pulled with ropes. Some people think that mud may have been used to make the surface slippery. The sleds moved by inches.

The sun was burning hot, but the men could not stop to rest. They were whipped if they did. Finally the heavy stones had to be lifted up and set into place. The work could break a man's back.

World's Largest Stone Building. These men were working on the Great Pyramid at Giza. It was, and still is, the largest

stone building in the world. It is made up of more than two million stone blocks, and it is as tall as a modern 35-story building. Five of Europe's largest cathedrals, including St. Peter's at Rome, could fit inside the area of its base. Suppose that its stones were cut into cubes measuring one foot by one foot. If placed in a row, these cubes would extend two thirds of the distance around the earth's equator.

Pyramids were built as tombs for Egypt's pharaohs. The pharaoh was considered to be a god who owned the nation and everything in it. Everyone in Egypt had to serve the god-king. The pharaoh Cheops (KEE-ops), who ruled from 2680-2657 B.C., drafted 100,000 workers a year to build the Great Pyramid. It took 20 years to finish.

How was the Great Pyramid built? First an area was chosen that was close to the Nile. This was because many of the huge building stones could only be transported from the quarries by ship. At flooding time, the distance between the Nile and the location of the pyramid was reduced to a quarter of a mile.

Mysterious Accuracy. The pyramid had to be built on a foundation of solid rock. So the next job of the builders was to remove the desert sand that covered the bedrock. Then the foundation had to be made level. How accurate were the ancient Egyptians in this operation? The base of the Great Pyramid was off level by only five eighths of an inch. This was the extremely small difference in height between the southeast corner and the northwest corner.

The next step was to make sure that the base of the pyramid formed a square that was near perfect. The measuring cords used by the builders were made of palm or flax fibers. Both of these fibers stretched when they were used. Despite this problem, the difference between the longest and shortest sides of the Great Pyramid was only 7.9 inches. As each side was more than 750 feet long, the error was remarkably small. Such accuracy could only have been achieved by the use of astronomy.

Meanwhile, other workers were cutting blocks from rocky desert cliffs. Sometimes they were a long way from Giza. Then the stones would be put on logs and rolled to the edge of the Nile. There they were loaded onto barges and rowed down the river. At Giza, they were mounted on sleds and pulled up ramps on each side of the pyramid. When put in place, each stone fit on top of the stone below.

The Great Pyramid was solid stone except for the pharaoh's room and the low, narrow tunnels leading to it. The tunnels were about a yard square. They were blocked with large stones so the pharaoh's mummy would be safe. But tomb robbers were able to break in. They stole the mummy to get its jewels.

Stairways to Heaven. Why did Cheops and other pharaohs build their tombs in the shape of pyramids? A sentence written in one of these tombs gives a clue. It

This painting shows Egyptians marching in a funeral procession. Could the objects they are carrying be intended for use in the next life?

says, "A staircase is laid for the pharaoh so that he may mount up to heaven on it." The pyramids, sloping high up to the sky, were "staircases to heaven." From them, Egyptians believed, the pharaohs could join the sun god, Re, and travel with him across the sky. Any time they wished, they could go back to their tombs. There, it was thought, they would enjoy the food and drink which was put out for them by the priests. Egypt's god-kings built the pyramids to use in their everlasting life after death.

✎ Quick Check

1. *Where are the pyramids located? What are they made of, and why were they built?*

2. *When and where was the Great Pyramid built? How does its size compare with modern buildings? Who ordered it to be built?*

3. *What is probably the method used to make sure the base of the Great Pyramid was level? How were the stones moved into place for the upper portions?*

4. *How were the pyramids supposed to be used by the pharaohs after their deaths?*

8
Hatshepsut: A Woman Rules

She was one of the most remarkable women the world has ever known. It was not enough for her to rule Egypt as Queen Hatshepsut (hat-SHEP-soot). She performed all the duties of a pharaoh. Why, then, shouldn't she be called pharaoh? It had never been done before, but that didn't stop Hatshepsut. One day she claimed that Amon, the greatest of Egypt's many deities, spoke to her inside his temple at Karnak. From the lips of the gold idol a voice said, "Go, my daughter, *king* of Egypt!"

In ancient Egypt, the pharaohs often claimed that the deities spoke to them. There was nothing unusual about that. But Hatshepsut was a woman, and she had powerful enemies. They protested that her story could not be believed. It was in vain. In the presence of great no-bles and priests, Hatshepsut placed on her head the double crown of upper and lower Egypt. She was the first woman ever to wear it. She also wore a gold beard that was attached to the crown. The beard, which was worn by all pharaohs, was a symbol of divine male power. She proclaimed throughout the land that all must call her *his* majesty. The exact year that she became King Hatshepsut is uncertain, but it was about 1500 B.C.

Hatshepsut's life story is told in her memorial temple at Thebes, the capital of ancient Egypt. Memorial temples were built by Egyptian kings as palaces to which their souls might return after death. Hers was cut deeply into a rocky cliff and was huge. It still stands today, and not even the passing of 3500 years

59

can mar its beauty. On its inner walls, the best artists of Hatshepsut's time carved and painted scenes from her life. Others carved the hieroglyphs that describe these scenes.

Hatshepsut claimed that she was of divine birth. In the first wall picture, the god Amon appears in the person of her father, King Thutmose I. The god-king tells her mother, Queen Amose, "Hatshepsut shall be the name of my daughter....She shall exercise the kingship in this whole land. My soul is hers, my will is hers, my crown is hers."

Father's Favorite. Hatshepsut was her father's favorite child, and he gave her the same training that was normally given to a royal son. As a young girl, she began wearing boys' clothes. Their chief feature was a brief, pleated kilt that ended at the knees. She is shown on a raft, spearing fish in the Nile. In another picture, she hurls nets to trap quail in the marshes. She also taunts a crocodile that is swimming among the reeds.

Hatshepsut had an older sister and two younger brothers, but they died when they were young. That left Hatshepsut as the sole heir to her father's throne. Thutmose was determined that she should succeed him. When Queen Amose died, Thutmose placed Hatshep-

Groomed to rule from birth and not content to be a mere queen, Hatshepsut became pharaoh of Egypt. During her reign (1500-1468 B.C.) Egypt enjoyed peace and a prosperous golden age.

sut beside him on the throne. He told the nobles and priests at his palace, "This is my daughter, Hatshepsut. Behold! I have appointed her my successor on the throne....She it is who shall lead you." Those who obeyed her, Thutmose said, would live and prosper. But those who spoke evil of her would be put to death by Amon, the lord of the gods. At this time, Hatshepsut was not yet 20 years old. She appears as a slender, graceful young woman, but she still wears, as always, masculine clothes.

After the death of Thutmose, Hatshepsut ruled Egypt alone for a time. She was the first woman to do so. But the law—and the wishes of the people—required her to marry in order to produce an heir. The man she agreed to marry was a half brother. He was one of many children born to lesser wives of Thutmose. In ancient Egypt, it was the custom of kings to have more than one wife. It was also customary for a king to marry a sister or a half sister to keep the "divine" blood line pure. The half brother whom Hatshepsut married became King Thutmose II. She became the Great Queen and Great Royal Wife. But the records indicate that Thutmose II was a passive king and that Hatshepsut still was in control of Egypt.

Her Rival. While Thutmose II lived, Hatshepsut's title remained Great Queen. But soon after his early death, she stunned Egypt by assuming the double crown and the role of pharaoh. Why did she do it? She and Thutmose had two children, both girls. However, Thutmose also had a son by a lesser wife named Isis who wanted her son to become king. Isis persuaded his father to name the boy as his successor. The boy, who later became Thutmose III, was also ambitious. He dreamed of becoming a great warrior-king and could not wait to take power.

Hatshepsut was not about to share the throne with her young stepson. To strengthen her position, she crowned herself King Hatshepsut. For years she kept him from the throne and limited his role to commander of Egypt's armies.

Success Brings Revenge. Hatshepsut used her power well. While she was on the throne, Egypt enjoyed a golden age of peace, trade, and prosperity. Its cities were alive with the construction of new temples, monuments, and other buildings. Artists were put to work depicting Hatshepsut and other great persons of the time. Hatshepsut had hundreds of statues of herself made in the form of a sphinx—her head united to the body of a lion. It made no difference to her that sphinxes were royal male images. She would not be outdone by any pharaoh. In most of her images, she wears the gold beard of Egyptian kings.

When Hatshepsut died in 1468 B.C.—some say she was murdered—her stepson took his revenge. He ordered his soldiers to destroy every reminder of her. Armed with axes, the soldiers smashed every one of the statues made of her. They vandalized the wall pictures in her temple and chiseled out her name from the writing. In place of her name, the name of Thutmose III was substituted.

Fortunately, the temple itself was spared, probably because the soldiers feared to wreck a building that was dedicated to Amon. Later the temple was buried by landslides and disappeared for centuries. When it was dug up in the present century, historians were able to reconstruct her life story. It is the story of a brave woman who dared to rule Egypt as a pharaoh.

✎ **Quick Check**

1. *What was unique about Hatshepsut's rule? Approximately when did she rule Egypt and for how long? Describe her reign.*

2. *Who was Thutmose I, and what role did he play in Hatshepsut's rise to power?*

3. *Who succeeded Hatshepsut? Who was he? How did he feel about Hatshepsut, and what did he do?*

4. *What is a sphinx? What did it represent? What did Hatshepsut do that challenged this?*

The Nile River played a part in the lives of many ancient Egyptians—kings, queens, and ordinary people alike. This tomb painting shows Egyptian families working together as a team to hunt geese along the Nile.

9
The Pharaoh Who Worshipped One God

Egyptians could not believe what was happening. The pharaoh Amenhotep (a-men-HOE-tep) IV was closing the great temple of Amon at Thebes. Amon was the supreme god of Egypt, the king of the gods. Now the pharaoh wanted to wipe out his name completely. Throughout Egypt, the pharaoh's men destroyed the name Amon on temple walls, tombs, and stone markers. Amenhotep even had them destroy any mention of "the gods."

There was only one true god, he proclaimed. This was the sun, the creator on whom all life depended. The sun god was represented by a symbol—a radiant disc with rays of light that ended in little hands. In Egypt, the sun disc was the Aten. Amenhotep wanted Egyptians to worship only the Aten, "the great living disc, lord of heaven and earth." To show how serious he was, the pharaoh changed his name to Akhenaten (a-keh-NAH-ten). It meant "the glorified spirit of the Aten."

In the fourteenth century B.C. Akhenaten proclaimed a religious revolution. For 2000 years, the people of Egypt had worshipped many deities. At first, they usually took the shape of animals. Among them were the cat-goddess Bast, the cobra-goddess Edjo, and the jackal-god Wepwawe. Later the Egyptians created new ones that were part animal and part human. Typical of them was Horus, who had the head of a falcon and the body of a man. Now Akhenaten was telling the Egyptians that all their old deities were false. They must worship instead a single, all-powerful god. Akhenaten was

In the fourteenth century B.C., the pharaoh Akhenaten revolutionized religion in Egypt when he proclaimed the supremacy of one god. As reflected in this carving, Akhenaten also changed art, calling for it to be realisitc, lively, and warm. Note the pharaoh (left), with Queen Nefertiti and three of their six daughters.

one of the first people ever to believe in one god.

At the time that Akhenaten was born, Egypt was a very rich and powerful land. Gold poured into it from the mines of the Sudan in the south. Tribute, or payment, came from foreign princes in Egypt's empire to the north. Akhenaten's father, Amenhotep III, and his mother, Queen Tiy, lived amid great luxury. Their palace at Thebes covered 80 acres. It had an artificial lake that was more than a mile long. Water from the Nile flowed into it by means of a canal.

Not much is known about Akhenaten's childhood. He does not appear on any of his father's monuments, perhaps because he was not good-looking. But his looks did not hinder Akhenaten after he became pharaoh. Then he married a beautiful young woman named Nefertiti (nef-er-TEE-tee). Her name, in fact, means "the beautiful one is come." Before long, she gave birth to a daughter, Merataten. Five other daughters would follow.

Where the young Akhenaten got his religious ideas is uncertain. The idea of a sun god, however, was nothing new. Egyptians had worshipped Re, god of the sun, since earliest times. Later they also began to worship the Aten, or sun disc. Even before the reign of Akhenaten, pharaohs were associated with it. Amenhotep III, Akhenaten's father, was called "the dazzling sun disc."

A New Capital. When Akhenaten became the pharaoh, he went one step further. Unlike his father, he had no use for Amon, the chief god of Egypt. One of his first acts was to build a temple devoted to the Aten at Thebes. This enraged the priests of the temple of Amon. For a while, however, Akhenaten did not interfere with the worship of Amon or any other deities. Then, in the sixth year of his rule, he made a startling break with the past. By that time, he could no longer tolerate Thebes, the city where Amon was chief god. He decided to create a new capital city that would be devoted solely to the Aten.

The city was built on barren land on the east bank of the Nile. It was midway between Thebes and Memphis (see map p. 51). The pharaoh named it Akhetaten, which means "the horizon of the sun disc." Today the site is known as Amarna (ah-MAR-nah). Here he wrote a great hymn to the Aten. It was inscribed on the tomb of one of his officials. A part of it, which has been edited, follows.

> You arise beauteous in the horizon of heaven, O living Aten, beginner of life. You banish darkness, and the earth grows bright. Egypt's hands are upraised in praise at your glorious appearing.
>
> The entire land now does its work. All cattle are at peace upon the pastures. Trees and pasture grow green. Birds take flight from their nests, and their wings give praise to your spirit. All animals frisk upon their feet. The fish in the river leap before your face. Every eye beholds you in front of it. You are the sole god. There is none other like you.

Queen Nefertiti was a lovely woman whose name means "the beautiful one is come." This bust comes from a full-size statue of the queen.

At Amarna, worship of the Aten took place in open courtyards, rather than enclosed temples. The god's presence was felt in the rays of the sun. Large crowds attended the services, but only Akhenaten and his family actually took part in them. Akhenaten prayed directly to the sun disc. Everyone else had to pray to Akhenaten. He was their only means of communicating with the Aten.

More Natural Art. Akhenaten was an unusual pharaoh in other ways. In the past, Egyptian artists portrayed the pharaohs as heroic figures. They are mighty hunters and warriors and have perfect physiques. They sat in stiff, formal poses, looking straight ahead. They are beautiful but unreal. Akhenaten wanted artists to show people as they really are, not as they ought to be.

Artists seem to have taken him at his word. Akhenaten does not look like a hero at all. Stone carvings and statues show him as an ugly, deformed man. His head is long and thin, his jaw and chin stick out. His shoulders are narrow, his chest is scrawny, and he has a potbelly. His hips are very wide, and his thighs heavy. From the knees down, his legs are skinny. He is never shown, as other pharaohs were, leading an army in battle. He is often shown lounging in a chair or eating at a table heaped with food and drink.

However, the scenes of the pharaoh with Nefertiti and their children are quite appealing. He and the queen look like loving parents as they embrace their children, or bounce them on their knees. The new art that Akhenaten brought about is known today as the Amarna style.

The change in art was to endure much longer than the change in religion. Akhenaten died in the seventeenth year of his reign. How he died is not known. Although his tomb was found, his mummy was not. Worship of the sun disc did not last very long after his death. The pharaohs who followed him restored the old deities. It is more than likely that most Egyptians were relieved. They were never really comfortable with the idea of one god.

Akhenaten's temples and other buildings were razed to the ground by his successors. They blamed him for the decline of Egypt's empire. He had ignored the deities, and they in turn abandoned Egypt. Eventually what remained of Amarna was buried under desert sands.

✎ Quick Check

1. *How did Akhenaten propose a religious revolution? What god did he want the people of Egypt to worship? What was the symbol of this god?*

2. *How was Egyptian art different in Akhenaten's time? What is the name given to its style? Where does its name come from?*

3. *Which change brought about by Akhenaten survived his reign? Which did not? What was the probable reaction of most Egyptians?*

Tutankhamen, a later pharaoh who revived the idealized style of Egyptian art, is shown with symbols of the god Osiris.

PART 2
Review and Skills Exercises

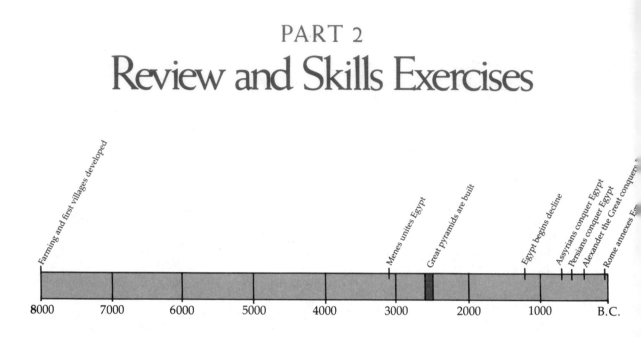

Timeline from 8000 B.C. to B.C. with markings at 7000, 6000, 5000, 4000, 3000, 2000, 1000.

Events on timeline:
- Farming and first villages developed
- Menes unites Egypt
- Great pyramids are built
- Egypt begins decline
- Assyrians conquer Egypt
- Persians conquer Egypt
- Alexander the Great conquers
- Rome annexes Eg

Understanding Events

You have read in Part 2 that Egypt was a united empire for almost 3000 years beginning with the reign of King Menes. The end of this long period was marked by unrest within Egypt and domination by different groups from outside Egypt. From approximately 700 B.C., Egypt was conquered by the Assyrians, the Persians, Alexander the Great of Macedonia, and the Romans. Study the time line above and answer the questions.

1. Which came first, the creation of farming villages or the uniting of the north and south under King Menes?

2. In what century did King Menes achieve his unification of north and south Egypt?

3. When were the pyramids built?

4. Refer to your text to answer the following: Where on the time line would you put the reign of Hatshepsut? The reign of Akhenaten?

5. According to the time line, did the Persians or Romans conquer Egypt first?

Comparing Civilizations

Your text contains this statement: "Unlike Sumerian cities, Egyptian cities could often work together." Write a brief explanation of the meaning of the statement. In your explanation include answers to these questions: What does the reference to Sumer mean? What was the result of Egyptian cities working together?

Interpreting a Reading

Read the information and answer the questions that follow.

The Rosetta Stone

Suppose you found a bottle with a message in it. When you opened it, you could not read the writing because you did not know the language. What would you do? You might try to find someone who spoke that language. But suppose there was no one alive who could speak it?

This happens all the time to people who study ancient languages. Every once in a while, though, they get lucky. Such was the case of the Rosetta Stone.

In 1799, a French soldier was investigating some ruins in a town on a branch of the Nile. He was serving under Napoleon, who occupied Egypt at that time. The town was named Rosetta. There, buried in the mud, he found a black rock almost four feet long and just over two feet wide. It was covered with writing.

When scholars studied the stone, they found that the same message was written in three different languages. One of them was ancient Greek. Since they could read this language, they were able to figure out the other two.

These languages were both Egyptian. One was hieroglyphics, the written language of Egyptian priests and scholars. The other writing was a simpler version of hieroglyphics. It was used by the common people. It was carved in a band around the middle of the stone. The hieroglyphics were at the top and the Greek at the bottom.

Until the Rosetta Stone was found, no one had been able to understand Egyptian writing. Now it was possible to understand all kinds of mysteries of ancient Egypt.

Later scholars were able to learn that the stone was carved about 195 B.C., during the reign of Ptolemy V Epiphanes.

The Rosetta Stone now stands in the British Museum in London. Its polished black, etched surface gives us a vital key to understanding the past.

1. Where was the Rosetta Stone found and by whom?
2. When was the stone carved? Was this date toward the beginning, middle, or end of ancient Egyptian civilization?
3. Explain the significance of the Rosetta Stone.
4. List any unfamiliar words in the reading. Write a dictionary definition for the words on the list.

Building Vocabulary

Below are four groups of words. Use the words in each group in a brief paragraph that describes some aspect of Egyptian history you have read about in Part 2. Each group of words should be used in a separate paragraph.

1. pyramids
   pharaohs
   mummies
   preserve
   vandalized

2. fortunate
   fertile
   dependent
   cooperate
   dikes
   prosper

3. afterlife
   everlasting
   memorial
   remarkable

4. jackal
   hieroglyphs
   graceful
   masculine

PART
3

THE
NEAR EAST

While the Assyrians were building an empire in Mesopotamia, three remarkable groups of people developed civilizations in the Near East. They were the Hittites, the Phoenicians, and the Hebrews.

What made these peoples remarkable? Each group made at least one important cultural, religious, or political achievement. These achievements still influence us.

By the time the Hittites built an empire in the Near East, human society was growing more complex. It was no longer possible for a group of people to settle in an area without the fear of attack by another people. The Hittites themselves were not brutal conquerors. But peoples such as the Assyrians stopped at nothing in order to gain new territory. The Hittites had to find ways to deal with the threat.

At first they simply found better ways to defend themselves. They learned how to get iron from iron ore and made powerful iron spears and hatchets. Other peoples used bronze, which was expensive, or stone, which could break. So successful were the Hittite weapons that they carefully guarded the secret of how they were made. Unfortunately for them, the Assyrians stole the secret. Eventually, most peoples learned how to use iron.

Then, about 1284 B.C., a great change came about. The Hittites decided not to fight their enemies alone. They asked the Egyptians for help against the Assyrians. Thus, a system of treaties was born. Nations now could cooperate with other nations instead of constantly fighting among themselves.

Hittite treaties were simple. The first recorded treaty simply was an agreement between the Hittites and Egyptians to defend each other in emergencies. Like some later treaties in history, the agreement was sealed with a royal marriage between the two nations. Hittite treaties sometimes included passionate threats designed to scare leaders into obeying them. "May the deities blot you out [if you break the treaty]" was a popular curse. Hittite treaties, carved in clay and stone, are some of the best-surviving records of ancient diplomacy.

Alphabet Invented. The Phoenicians (foe-NEE-shunz) left very different kinds of records. They wrote down the details of trade in a form of writing that they invented. This was the alphabet. Unlike the cuneiform and hieroglyphics invented in Sumer and Egypt, the letters of the Phoenician alphabet represented the sounds of the human voice. This made it much easier to read and write, and many more people could learn. The word *alphabet* comes from the Phoenician *aleph* and *beth*, their first two letters. Later, the Greeks would adopt the Phoenician alphabet, and it greatly influenced our modern alphabet.

The Phoenicians were not empire-builders. They lived in small city-states on the shores of the Mediterranean. Carthage, Tyre, and Sidon were some of their greatest cities. Instead of farming, they became wealthy by trading with Mediterranean countries and with peoples as far away as West Africa. So wealthy were they that they literally paid other nations not to invade their territory.

Like the Hittites, the Phoenicians had many deities. Their deities were even more fearsome than the Hittites'. In Carthage especially, it was believed that the deities had to be "fed" with human and animal sacrifices. Sacrifices of babies, children, and young animals were widespread. The pagan religions of both these peoples did not include even the most basic morality. However, there was one group of people of this period whose religion included a strict code of moral behavior. These were the Hebrews, who lived in a small area that is now Israel and part of Jordan. Their descendants are called Jews.

The Hebrews were neither empire-builders nor great merchants. They were slaves in Egypt for centuries. After they were freed, they were only united as a nation for a short while. They could not even protect their lands from invaders. What made them remarkable? They were the first *monotheistic* people. This meant that they only worshipped one deity, in their case a god.

Like most religions, the Hebrew religion developed over a long period. We can divide this time into three stages. At the first stage, the god was named Yahweh (YAH-way). He looked like a man. He was often very emotional and had complete power over the people who worshipped him. This god was often, but not always, wise. He would punish someone who committed a sin by accident just as quickly as someone who committed a sin on purpose. One sin was speaking the name Yahweh. He was only to be called God.

Although they had only one god, the Hebrews at the first stage did not differ much from other peoples in their patterns of worship. They sacrificed animals and performed many rituals.

At the second stage of religious development, the Hebrews began to believe that it was important to have a pure heart and not commit any sins. Sins were defined in the Ten Commandments, which, according to the Old Testament, God gave to a leader called Moses. The commandments were laws that defined murder, envy, and adultery, among other things, as sins.

The Hebrew God had limited power. He only ruled over the Hebrews. However, a great change was coming in the Hebrew religion. In the eighth and seventh centuries B.C., several Hebrew prophets began to preach reform. God no longer wanted his followers to make sacrifices and perform rituals. He no longer made errors in judging people. God was now considered the ruler of all people, even pagans. But he did not have complete power over them. Rather, people were allowed to make their own mistakes. And God only created good things. Any evil in the world came from people, not God.

With the new religious beliefs came a new commitment to good and moral behavior. It was no longer enough to simply obey the Ten Commandments. Instead, the Hebrews created laws that were supposed to be a reflection of God's will. These laws were more humane than any the world had ever seen. One of them commanded that people be charitable to the poor and strangers. Another law said that all slaves would be set free after they had served for six years. A third law forbade punishing children for the crimes their parents had committed.

Morally, the Hebrews set an example for the rest of the ancient world. But they did not influence most of the peoples around them. Christianity, which developed many centuries after the fall of the Hebrew nations, was the first religion to use Hebrew beliefs and law. The religion of Islam also has its roots in the Hebrew faith.

Today, when you read of a new treaty, or hear someone sound out a word "phonetically", or hear one of the Ten Commandments, you can think of these three peoples of the Near East.

MAP EXERCISE

This map shows the Hittite Empire in 1450 B.C. Use it to answer the following questions:

1. What river flowed along the eastern border of the Hittite Empire? What body of water lay to the south of it?

2. Name two civilizations located south of the Hittite Empire.

3. How far would a Hittite ship have to sail to get to the nation with which the Hittites signed their first peace treaty?

THE HITTITE EMPIRE

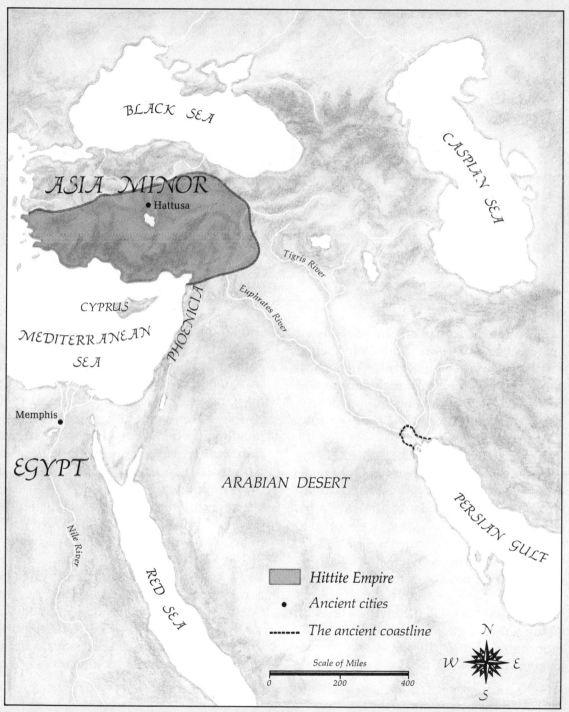

BLACK SEA

CASPIAN SEA

ASIA MINOR

• Hattusa

Tigris River

Euphrates River

CYPRUS

MEDITERRANEAN
SEA

PHOENICIA

Memphis •

EGYPT

ARABIAN DESERT

PERSIAN GULF

Nile River

RED SEA

	Hittite Empire
•	Ancient cities
-------	The ancient coastline

Scale of Miles

0   200   400

N
W   E
S

10
The Hittites:
An Ironclad Empire

They built a great empire that lasted for hundreds of years. They boldly challenged the power of Egypt. Then, suddenly and mysteriously, their empire was destroyed. They vanished from history. Not until recent times were these people, the Hittites, rediscovered.

In 1906, archaeologists unearthed the ruins of the capital city of the Hittite empire. Called Hattusa, it was located about 90 miles east of Ankara, the capital of modern Turkey. It was a well-fortified city surrounded by stone walls up to 26 feet thick. If you walked around these walls, you would cover four miles.

Hattusa itself was a natural stronghold. It stood 3000 feet above sea level on a rugged plateau and was ringed by mountains. From this base, which was known as the land of Hatti, the Hittites spread out and brought many people under their rule. Hittite kings liked to negotiate with other rulers rather than conquer them. If they accepted the Hittite kings as their rulers, they and their people were granted much freedom. The relationship between Hatti and a subject state was written out in a treaty. In other parts of the Near East, treaties were almost unknown.

The Hittite empire was established by 1750 B.C. It was the first powerful society to arise outside of the fertile river valleys of the Near East. At its height, it was as large as modern France and England combined. It stretched from the Aegean Sea on the west to upper Mesopotamia on the east (see map p. 75). On the north it reached almost to the Black Sea. On the south it bordered the Mediterranean Sea.

Where the Hittites came from is another mystery. They were not kin to the people of Mesopotamia and others in the Near East. They spoke a language that may have come from southern Russia. Historians believe that they moved into Asia Minor (modern Turkey) over a long period of time. Gradually they came to rule over the people they found there.

The Hittites absorbed much of the culture of the Near East. They learned the cuneiform writing of Mesopotamia and used it along with their own hieroglyphic writing. They also adopted many of its gods and goddesses. In all, the Hittites had as many as 1000 deities.

At Hattusa, archaeologists found many clay tablets on which Hittite kings wrote the history of their reigns. Many of them were in the language of Babylonia, which historians could read. But they could not read the hieroglyphic writing of the Hittites. There was only one way to solve the puzzle. They would have to find a record written in two languages, Hittite and another that they understood. By comparing the two, they would be able to solve the Hittite hieroglyphs.

Not until after World War II did historians get what they needed. Then archaeologists uncovered stones with writing in both Hittite hieroglyphs and Phoenician. An expert in Phoenician, who was familiar with the Hittite hieroglyphs, solved the puzzle in his sleep. When he woke up, he was able to match the words in both languages.

Appeal for Understanding. The records left by the Hittite kings are quite unusual. They often try to justify their actions and seem to ask readers for approval. In the thirteenth century B.C., for example, King Mursili III lost his throne in a revolt. It was led by Mursili's uncle, who crowned himself King Hattusili III (1289-1265 B.C.). The new king "speaks" to readers in the following words, which have been edited.

For seven years I conformed to Mursili's rule. But he sought to destroy me. Then I no longer conformed, but broke with him. All the same, I did not do so treacherously. Instead, I declared war on him openly. I wrote to him and said, "You have picked a quarrel with me. You are the great king, while I possess only one small stronghold that you left me. Well, the deities will decide between us!"

Some people might say, "It was you who placed him on the throne in the first place. Why did you then depose him?" My answer is, "If he had not picked a quarrel with me, would the deities have permitted a great king to be defeated by a little king?" It is because he picked a quarrel with me that the deities brought him to defeat at my hands.

Mursili fled to Egypt, where he was protected by the pharaoh, Ramses II. Hattusili demanded that the pharaoh return Mursili to him, but Ramses refused. Then the Hittite king complained, "When I wrote to him [Ramses], to send me my enemy, he did not send him. Therefore the king of Egypt and I are angry with each other."

A Showdown. Relations between the Hittites and Egypt had been strained for many years. During the reign of the pharaoh, Akhenaton (about 1375-1358 B.C.), Egypt was torn by religious upheavals (see chapter 9). The Hittites took advantage of Egypt's weakness to expand their empire into northern Syria. Egypt had long ruled Syria and regarded the Hittites as troublemakers. In 1301 B.C., the young pharaoh Ramses II began attacking the Hittites there. This made the Hittite king Muwatilli furious. He raised a large army for a battle against Egypt. Whoever won would become the supreme power in the Near East.

The battle took place in the spring of 1300 B.C. at Kadesh in Syria. According to Egyptian records, about 40,000 troops took part in it. At the outset, the Hittites drew the Egyptians into a trap. Ramses' forces were cut to pieces by the Hittites' three-man chariots. Fortunately for Ramses, the Hittite chariot soldiers could not resist looting the Egyptian camp. While this was going on, fresh Egyptian troops arrived. Now Ramses bravely counterattacked, and the Hittites also suffered heavy losses. Later Ramses boasted that he had won a great victory at Kadesh. At most, it was a moral victory. Historians believe that Ramses and

The Hittites were known for making treaties, but they fought battles, too. They used chariots like the one in this lion hunt (below). Page 70: Ancient Persia's greatest city was Persepolis, where a royal palace once stood.

the remainder of his army were lucky to have escaped with their lives.

First Treaty. For years after the battle, the two empires were enemies, but they did not go to war again. Meanwhile both were becoming alarmed by the growing power of Assyria, a kingdom in northern Mesopotamia. The Assyrian king regarded himself as the equal of the Egyptian and Hittite rulers. At this point, distrust of Assyria led Ramses II and Hattusili III to put aside their differences. In 1284 B.C., 16 years after the battle of Kadesh, the two rulers signed a treaty that made them allies. They agreed

- not to make war on each other,
- to come to each other's aid in case of an attack by another kingdom,
- to respect each other's borders and empires.

This treaty brought peace to the Near East. It was one of the first mutual defense treaties ever signed by two great powers.

The alliance between the Hittites and Egypt was later made stronger by a royal wedding. A daughter of Hattusili became the bride of Ramses II. Both rulers were very pleased. Hattusili referred to Ramses as "the Great King of Egypt." The pharaoh was delighted with "this fine decision to let the two countries forever become one single country."

The alliance lasted as long as the Hittite empire did—until 1200 B.C. At that time, the Hittite empire was swiftly destroyed. Hattusa was burned to the ground. The marks of fire can still be seen on the city's walls. Other Hittite cities were also put to the torch. The people scattered, and the great urban centers with their palaces and temples became ghost towns.

Who destroyed the land of Hatti? Historians can only guess, because Hittite records end in 1200 B.C. One guess is that the empire was overrun by the "sea peoples." They were attackers who poured into the Near East from Greece and the Aegean Islands around this time. Egyptian records from the reign of Ramses III show how much they were feared. "The foreign countries plotted on their island homelands. No land could stand before their arms, beginning with Hatti . . . ."

A proud people and a great empire vanished. They would not be rediscovered until 3000 years later.

✎ Quick Check

1. *Where was the land of Hatti? What were its boundaries? Name its capital. How long did it flourish and when?*

2. *What was unusual about the writings of the Hittite kings? How did the Hittites like to deal with the people they conquered?*

3. *Where and when was the famous battle fought between Egypt and the Hittites? What was the outcome?*

4. *What brought Egypt and the Hittites together? How did they seal their alliance? What made it even stronger?*

5. *What is one explanation for the end of the Hittite Empire?*

11
The Phoenicians

The Phoenicians were the greatest sailors, adventurers, and traders of their time. For 300 years, their ships carried much of the trade in the Mediterranean Sea. They brought the fine goods of the Middle East and Egypt to the peoples of Europe. They also gave the Europeans something even more valuable. This was the alphabet, which they probably adapted from earlier Middle Eastern languages.

The Phoenicians occupied a narrow strip of land on the east coast of the Mediterranean. They lived in a number of independent city-states that were ruled by kings. The most important of these kingdoms were Tyre and Sidon. At times, one kingdom would dominate the rest. But they never united as a nation.

The Phoenician city-states were in an area that today is mainly Lebanon. In front of them was the sea. Behind them were high mountains. There was little land for farming. So the Phoenicians turned to the Mediterranean as a way of making a living.

At first they sailed their small ships close to shore by day. At night they put their ships on beaches. But later they built larger ships and learned to sail at night by the stars.

Exploring and Trading. By 1100 B.C. they were masters of the sea. They began sailing boldly to strange lands. They sailed to Greece, Italy, North Africa, Spain, Britain, and the west coast of Africa. They started colonies or trading posts in all of these places.

As explorers of the ancient world, the Phoenicians were second to none. Their furthest journey was made about 600 B.C. The ancient Greek historian Herodotus says that it was made for the Egyptian pharaoh Necho. The pharaoh wanted to

prove that Africa was surrounded by sea except where it meets Asia. (This is the land bridge which is now cut through by the Suez canal.) Necho hired Phoenician sailors and ships to sail down the Red Sea and around the tip of Africa. At the Pillars of Hercules (now the Straits of Gibraltar), they were to enter the Mediterranean. Sailing along the coast of North Africa, they would return to Egypt.

Herodotus says that it took the Phoenicians more than two years to make the journey. They were not sailing continuously, however. Each fall they would go ashore, plant crops, and wait to harvest them. When the food was taken aboard, they would continue their voyage.

The Phoenicians were not looking for glory. They were looking for trade. Often they did not understand the language of the people they met. But that did not stop the Phoenicians from making deals. Herodotus tells how the Phoenicians traded in West Africa:

When they arrive, they unload their goods [that they want to sell] on the beach. Then they go back to their ship and send up a smoke signal. The natives see the smoke and come down to the shore. They then put down as much gold as they think the goods are worth. The Phoenicians come ashore and look at the gold. If they think the gold is enough, they take it and go their way. But if it does not seem enough, they go back to their ship and wait. Then the natives approach and add to the gold until the Phoenicians are content. Both sides are fair. The Phoenicians never touch the gold until it matches the worth of their goods. And the natives never carry off the goods until the gold is taken away.

Swapping Products and Ideas. Phoenician ships carried all kinds of cargo. Wood from the famous cedar forests of Lebanon was shipped to Egypt and other neighboring countries. Phoenician cloth was also carried abroad. It was often tinted with a purple dye that only the Phoenicians could supply. This dye was made from a kind of shellfish known as *murex*. The dead murex gives off a liquid that was used to color white cloth anywhere from rose to dark purple. The darkness of the shade depended on how long the liquid was exposed to the sun. The method was to break the shells, take out the fish, and put them in vats. Dye "factories" were kept away from Phoenician cities because of their unpleasant odor. Today huge heaps of shells can be found in the area of Tyre and Sidon. The

MAP EXERCISE

The land of Palestine included the states of Israel and Judah. Compare this map with a modern map of the Middle East. Use them to answer the following:

1. What two cities were part of ancient Phoenicia? In what country or countries are these same two cities found today?

2. The empire of David and Solomon spread to what river to the northeast? What other river flowed through the empire?

3. After 922 B.C., which of the three was smallest in area: Phoenicia, Israel, or Judah? Which had the shortest coastline?

ANCIENT PHOENICIA AND PALESTINE

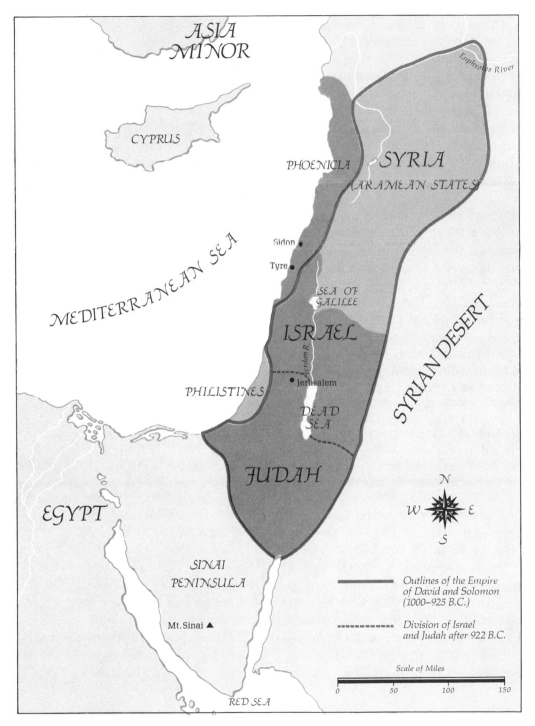

ASIA MINOR

CYPRUS

PHOENICIA

SYRIA
(ARAMEAN STATES)

Euphrates River

MEDITERRANEAN SEA

Sidon •

Tyre •

SEA OF GALILEE

ISRAEL

Jordan R.

SYRIAN DESERT

PHILISTINES

• Jerusalem

DEAD SEA

JUDAH

EGYPT

N
W   E
S

SINAI PENINSULA

Mt. Sinai ▲

Outlines of the Empire of David and Solomon (1000–925 B.C.)

Division of Israel and Judah after 922 B.C.

Scale of Miles

0   50   100   150

RED SEA

murex, though, is almost extinct there because so many were fished in ancient times.

The Phoenicians were also known for their metal products such as decorated bowls and jugs and precious jewelry. Copper for pots came from Cyprus. Silver and gold came from Ethiopia. Phoenician ships sailed to the west coast of Africa and to India to obtain metals and ivory.

The Phoenicians were for centuries the outstanding traders of the ancient world. The ancient historian Josephus described the trade between Phoenicia and Israel when King Solomon was building his palace and temple. The following quotation from Josephus has been edited.

> These works Solomon completed in 20 years. Hiram, the king of Tyre, contributed much gold and more silver to their building. He also contributed wood of cedar and pine trees. In return, Solomon presented Hiram with great gifts. Every year he sent Hiram grain and wine and olive oil. Because Tyre was situated on an island, Hiram had great need of these products.

The Phoenicians were good businessmen and kept careful records of their deals. But to do this, they had to have a good system of writing. Both the Egyptian and Sumerian systems were hard to learn and use. So the Phoenicians adapted another system, which contained an alphabet. Their letters, much changed in form, make up most of the alphabet that we use today. The Phoeni-

Cedar wood from Lebanon was among the cargo Phoenician ships carried.

cians taught this alphabet to the Greeks, who added the vowel letters to it. This simple alphabet spread the art of writing in the Western world.

✎ Quick Check

1. *Where was the Phoenicians' home base? What might have caused them to turn to the sea for their livelihood?*

2. *Why did the Phoenicians sail all the way around Africa? Who hired them to do it? How long did it take and why?*

3. *Describe a typical trade between the Phoenicians and the Africans. Name some of the products the Phoenicians traded throughout the ancient world and where these products came from.*

4. *What great contribution did the Phoenicians pass on to the Europeans? Where did the Phoenicians get it? Why did they need it?*

12
Israel: A New Faith out of the Desert

The land of Israel in ancient times was a bridge between two great civilizations, Egypt and Mesopotamia. It was crossed by travelers, traders, soldiers, priests, and princes.

This narrow strip of land between the Mediterranean Sea and the Jordan River was dwarfed by the powerful empires that it linked. It had a small population and few natural resources. Its people never stood out among the great builders or warriors of the ancient world. While only the ruins of ancient Egypt and Mesopotamia survive today, Israel's influence on the modern world is vast.

What accounts for this? The people who lived there, called Hebrews, were unique among the peoples of the Near East. Their way of life produced three great religions: the Jewish, the Christian, and the Muslim. The experiences of the ancient Hebrews are told in the Bible. No other book has had so great an impact on Western civilization. Its moral teachings and its belief in one God are shared by many nations and millions of people.

The nation and the faith of ancient Israel developed over many centuries. The Hebrews first appear in history about 1800 B.C. At that time, they were a nomadic people. They wandered with their herds from one desert oasis to another in the Near East. Like other desert nomads, they were attracted by the fertile lands closer to the Mediterranean Sea. They began to settle in the coastal region that was known as Canaan. There they organized themselves into 12 tribes.

Canaan was part of the Fertile Crescent and usually had a good supply of water.

85

Enslaved in Egypt, Hebrews were forced to do hard labor (above), including building cities for such pharaohs as Ramses II (shown in statue at right).

Yet there were occasional periods of drought that led to famine. At such times the various tribes would migrate to Egypt. There the annual flooding of the Nile and the system of irrigation canals provided a more dependable water supply.

Flight to Egypt. Sometime in the late seventeenth century, B.C., Canaan suffered a long drought. Many Hebrews began moving into Egypt as far as the Nile Delta. The Egyptians usually did not wel-come foreigners. But now they had no control over the delta region. Egypt had been invaded earlier by a warlike people from the East called Hyksos. The name means "rulers from foreign countries." The Hyksos traveled a lot and were among the first to use horse-drawn chariots in warfare. They conquered northern Egypt about 1720 B.C. and ruled it for a century and a half. They were finally driven out of Egypt by Pharaoh Ahmose I (1575-1550 B.C.).

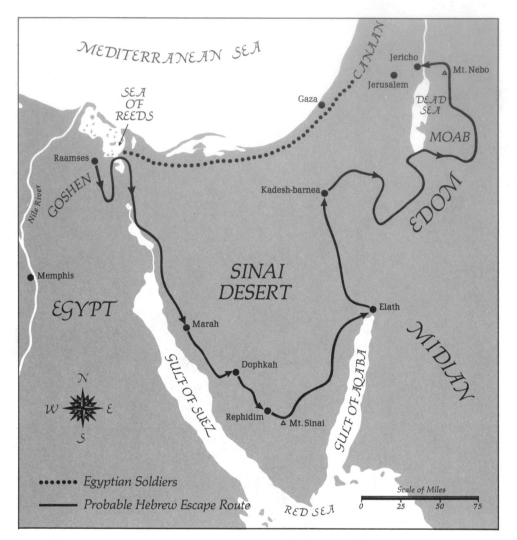

Egyptian Soldiers
Probable Hebrew Escape Route

MAP EXERCISE

After leaving Egypt, the Hebrews wound their way through the desert before reaching their destination. Use the map to answer the following questions:

1. In which direction is Canaan from Egypt?

2. As the Hebrews journeyed back to Canaan, what kind of land were they crossing?

3. What body of water did the Hebrews cross? At what point were they farthest from any body of water?

The war against the Hyksos made the Egyptians hostile to outsiders. Those foreigners who had not fled the country were made slaves. They were forced to do hard labor for the pharaohs. One of them, Ramses II (1290-1224 B.C.), ordered the building of new cities. Slave labor was used to get them completed quickly. The Hebrews were among those who felt the whip of Egyptian taskmasters.

Despite a long period of slavery, the Hebrews did not give up hope of becoming free. Late in the thirteenth century B.C., a group of them united to plan an escape from Egypt. They chose as their leader Moses who, the Bible says, was raised in the court of the pharaoh.

The Exodus. Some scholars have been troubled by the fact that Moses is not mentioned in Egyptian records. Neither is the escape of the Hebrews which he led. Other scholars, however, have no doubt that the story of the Exodus (going out) from Egypt is basically true. The name Moses is Egyptian and is similar to the names of several pharaohs. Among them are Thutmose and Ahmose.

Why wasn't the Exodus mentioned in Egyptian records? The Egyptians were a proud people. When they lost a battle, they either called it a victory or did not record it at all. Even the long rule of the Hyksos was not mentioned until they were expelled. It is also possible that the escape of the Hebrews was not considered very important by the Egyptian government.

Lesson in the Desert. The escape from Egypt was very important, however, to the Hebrews and the future of Western civilization. They escaped to the Sinai desert, across the Red Sea from Egypt. While they were struggling to survive in the desert, their faith became more important to them. It was here that the Hebrews received the Ten Commandments from Moses and pledged to obey them. They did not doubt that these commandments were given to Moses by God. This is what they say.

1. You shall have no other gods before me.

2. You shall not make any pictures, statues, or images for the purposes of worship.

3. You shall not take the name of the Lord your God in vain.

4. Remember the Sabbath day to keep it holy.

5. Honor your father and mother.

6. You shall not commit murder.

7. You shall not commit adultery.

8. You shall not steal.

9. You shall not bear false witness against your neighbor.

10. You shall not desire what belongs to your neighbor.

The Ten Commandments became the foundation of the Hebrews' faith. They demanded ethical, or moral, behavior on

Moses led the Hebrews out of Egypt and helped them found a new faith while in the Sinai Desert. In this wall sculpture he is shown receiving the Ten Commandments from the hand of God.

the part of every person. They also affirmed the Hebrews' commitment to *monotheism*, the belief in only one God. The Hebrews thought of the Ten Commandments as a *covenant*, or binding agreement, between them and their Lord. They would worship only God and obey these commandments. In return, God would protect them. Eventually monotheism and ethical behavior would become the basis of the Christian and Muslim faiths as well.

Is it possible that Moses' belief in one God was influenced by the pharaoh, Akhenaten (see chapter 9)? More than 100 years before the Exodus, Akhenaten had worshipped the sun disc as the sole creator and ruler of the world. He had tried to stamp out all the other gods that Egyptians worshipped. But there were important differences between the monotheism of Akhenaten and that of Moses. Worship of the sun disc was not related

to ethical behavior. Also, as the sun disc's priest on earth, Akhenaten considered himself a god. It may be said that the pharaoh actually approved of two gods — the sun disc and himself. Moses, on the other hand, never considered himself a god.

✎ Quick Check

1. Where was ancient Israel? What was the area called? What was the livelihood of its people? Why did they migrate to Egypt?

2. How were the Hebrews treated in Egypt? What was the Exodus?

3. Who was Moses? What were the laws that he gave to the Hebrews called? What was the covenant between the Hebrews and their god?

4. What three great religions can trace their origins to the Hebrews?

5. What previous Egyptian leader had worshipped only one god? How did his ideas differ from those of Moses?

This carving shows a menorah, a candle holder used in Jewish rituals.

13
A Prophet Sounds a Warning

Where would the Hebrew tribes go once they left the Sinai Desert? There was little doubt where they wanted to settle. Canaan was the land of their ancestors. It was the land, they believed, that God had promised them in return for their devotion.

Before they could settle in Canaan, however, they would have to conquer it. At this time, Canaan was occupied by people who engaged in farming and worshipped nature gods and goddesses.

The conquest of Canaan, which was led at first by Joshua, took place over a long period. The struggle was decided about 1125 B.C. when the Hebrews won a major victory over the Canaanites. It took place in the valley of Jezreel. But some Hebrew tribes refused to fight. This lack of unity continued even after the Hebrews occupied most of Canaan. Not until a great danger arose about a century later were the tribes able to unite against a common enemy.

Tribes Unite under Saul. When the Hebrews finally united, it was to resist an unusually strong group of invaders. They swept into the Near East from the Aegean Sea some time before 1200 B.C. They destroyed the Hittite empire, but were driven back from Egypt by the pharaoh, Ramses III (1182-1151 B.C.). In Canaan, some of them settled along the coast and then began to push inland. They were called Philistines (FIL-eh-steenz). Much later, the Romans called this region Palestine, after the Philistines.

Soon the Philistines began to fight with the Hebrews. The invaders were tough, and they had the advantage of using iron weapons. The Hebrew tribes had to unite against the Philistines or be destroyed. In this situation, they chose a king to rule them. The Bible says that the Hebrews were warned against such a move by the prophet Samuel.

In ancient Israel, a prophet was a highly respected moral leader. These were not simply people who predicted the future. Samuel told the Hebrew leaders that they might someday be enslaved by powerful kings. But they rejected his warning. The man they chose as king was a soldier named Saul. The Bible says that he "was taller than any of the people." For the first time in their history, the 12 tribes of Israel were united under a *monarch,* or king.

At this time, Saul had no palace, no court, and no capital city. Yet he was a good leader. He formed large armies to drive away Israel's enemies. He defeated invaders from the East. Then he drove the Philistines back to their coastal cities to the west.

Later two opponents weakened his position. One was Samuel. The other was a young warrior named David. In a battle against the Philistines, David was credited with slaying their powerful leader, Goliath, in a one-on-one fight. This made David a great hero. At first, Saul showed his admiration for David by giving him his daughter Michal in marriage. But as David's popularity grew, Saul became suspicious of him. The Bible says that he drove David away from his court and then sent men to kill him.

David found safety among the hills of Judah. They were a favorite hiding place for rebels and outlaws. There he formed a private army of several hundred men and openly challenged Saul. The Philistines sensed that Saul's power was slipping. They decided to attack him. The Philistine army assembled in the valley of Jezreel. Saul rushed there with his forces to oppose them. In the battle that followed, the Philistines crushed the Hebrews, leaving thousands of them dead on the field. Saul himself was wounded. Rather than let the Philistines capture him, he committed suicide by falling on his sword.

David's Rise. The death of Saul left Israel without a leader and close to collapse. A power struggle soon developed between David and one of Saul's sons. David won and was made king about 1000 B.C.. He now began a series of conquests that made Israel the greatest power in the Near East. He threw out the Philistines, who never threatened Israel again. He subdued the regions around Israel. In time, he ruled an empire that stretched from the Sinai peninsula almost as far east as the Euphrates River.

Today David is remembered more as a builder and a champion of the God of Israel than as a general. One of his first acts as king was to seize the hill town, Jebus, which was occupied by a group of

Canaanites. Jebus was more or less central to the 12 tribes of Israel. David made it his capital. It soon became known as Jerusalem, and also as the City of David. In time, it would become one of the most influential cities in all history.

To arouse enthusiasm, David wanted to make the city a great religious center. He arranged to have the sacred Ark of the Covenant brought to Jerusalem. The Ark was a portable shrine that the Hebrews believed held the spirit of their God. It had been taken by the Philistines in 1050 B.C., but later was recaptured by the Hebrews. On the day that it was brought to Jerusalem on an oxcart, David ordered a great parade to celebrate the occasion. Tens of thousands of happy Hebrews marched in the procession. David led the parade, sometimes singing and dancing before the oxcart. From that day on, Jerusalem would be the religious center for the entire kingdom.

The Price. Not all was glorious during the reign of David. The Hebrews paid a high price for the new monarchy. David's building programs, his large army, and his lavish court cost a lot of money. It was necessary to tax the people heavily. The government also introduced forced labor. Every able-bodied man could be made to work for the government without pay. Toward the end of David's reign, David's favorite son, Absolom, led one of a series of uprisings. The rebellion was crushed, and Absolom was put to death by one of David's generals.

Solomon's Rule. Before David died, he named his son Solomon his successor. When Solomon became king, about 961 B.C., he made Jerusalem an even greater city. He built costly palaces and govern-

ment buildings, creating an imposing capital. His most famous project was the temple that he had built to house the Ark of the Covenant. It was magnificent, but its cost was enormous. To pay for it, Solomon had to tax the people mercilessly. Tens of thousands of his subjects were forced to serve in labor gangs. Samuel's prophesy, that a powerful king would enslave the people, was coming true.

95

Solomon's rule brought great honor to the throne, but it also created great hostility. When Solomon died, about 928 B.C., the people were seething with resentment. They began to separate into tribes again. The 10 northern tribes, furious at Solomon's rule, would not accept his son as their king. Finally the northern tribes split away from the two southern tribes. The northern Hebrews called their new state the kingdom of Israel. The southern Hebrews called theirs the kingdom of Judah. The name came from the tribe of Judah, and from that name came the word "Jew." The two kingdoms would never unite again.

✎ Quick Check

1. *Where was the "promised land"? Why was it given this name?*

2. *What powerful invaders finally caused the Hebrew tribes to unite? When? Who led the Hebrews against them? What happened to him?*

3. *What was the meaning of the word "prophet" to the Hebrews? What was Samuel's warning? How did it seem to come true?*

4. *How did David become famous? When did he rule? How far did his empire reach? What was the name of his city?*

5. *Who ruled after David? What did he accomplish? What price did the Hebrews pay? What is the origin of the word "Jew"?*

By the time Solomon became king of Israel, Hebrews were using chariots drawn by horses and mules for both farming and war.

14
Divided They Fell

The breakup of Solomon's kingdom came at a time when both Egypt and Mesopotamia were again becoming warlike. They had armies that were much stronger than any that David had faced. The kingdoms of Israel and Judah had little rest. They were attacked almost constantly. However, they continued to develop their culture and religion.

In about 920 B.C., the Egyptian pharaoh, Shishak, invaded Judah with an army that included many Libyans and Ethiopians. They captured one town after another, and finally invaded the capital, Jerusalem. There, the soldiers plundered Solomon's temple and his palace. When they had everything they wanted, the army left and tried to invade Israel. Fortunately, the pharaoh had to recall his army because of problems at home. But the invasion clearly revealed just how weak the divided kingdom was.

Assyria Rules. The greatest threat to the Hebrews, though, did not come from Egypt in the west. It came from the east, from the growing power of Assyria. The Assyrians were powerful and experienced warriors (see chapter 5). In 853 B.C, the Hebrews were forced to fight the Assyrian army. King Ahab of Israel managed to hold it off for a time with 2,000 chariots and 10,000 foot soldiers. Eventually, though, Assyria conquered both kingdoms. The Assyrian soldiers did not destroy property or kill people. Instead, they forced them to pay yearly tributes of goods and money to the Assyrian kings.

The downfall of Israel came soon after its king, Hoshea (ho-SHEE-ah), defied Assyria. He refused to pay the yearly

An Assyrian pillar shows a king of Israel kneeling before king Shalmanesser III of Assyria. The Assyrians, among other conquerors, often made the reluctant Hebrews kneel to foreign deities.

tribute and tried to get Egypt to form an alliance against Assyria. Outraged, the Assyrians decided to crush Israel once and for all. They surrounded the capital of Israel, Samaria, for three years. Eventually, in 722 B.C. the Assyrians broke into the city. Their king, Sargon II, took great pride in his army's victory. He boasted that he sent more than 27,000 Hebrew prisoners to other parts of his empire. In time, these exiles became known as "the 10 lost tribes of Israel." Actually, they were not "lost." They were simply absorbed by the people among whom they were forced to resettle. But the kingdom of Israel had come to an

end. It became a colony of Assyria.

What happened to the kingdom of Judah? It managed to survive for more than a century after the fall of Israel, but it was ruled over by Assyria. In time, however, the Assyrian Empire began to crumble. By the end of the seventh century B.C., the Assyrian king was overthrown (see chapter 5). The Chaldeans succeeded the Assyrians and began to rebuild the Babylonian empire. They were the new masters of the Fertile Crescent.

To the Hebrews, one foreign master was as bad as another. In 589 B.C., they rebelled against their Babylonian overlords. The Babylonian king, Nebuchad-

In 589 B.C. Babylonian armies stormed Jerusalem and took many Hebrew prisoners. The wall carving above gives an idea of how the capture of Jerusalem might have looked.

99

This carving shows Hebrew prisoners being forced from Israel into exile.

nezzar (neh-boo-kad-NEZZ-er), struck back furiously. His armies destroyed all the fortified cities of Judah. Jerusalem was plundered and burned, and the Temple of Solomon was completely destroyed. Nebuchadnezzar was determined to prevent any more revolts. Many thousands of Judah's leading citizens — landowners, merchants, scholars, and skilled artisans — were taken to Babylon as captives. Only the poorest people of Judah were allowed to remain. The "promised land" was now a colony of Babylonia, ruled by Nebuchadnezzar and those who came after him.

Prophets Blame Corruption. The conquest of Israel and Judah raised serious questions among the Hebrews. They had made a covenant with their God a long time ago. They would worship God alone and obey God's commandments. In return, God would protect the "chosen people" and reward them with peace and prosperity. Why, then, had God allowed them to be conquered by people who worshipped false deities? Was it possible that the deities of Assyria and Babylonia were more powerful than the God of Israel?

A number of remarkable prophets tried to answer these questions. God, they said, had not abandoned the Hebrews. Rather, they had dishonored God by not obeying the Ten Commandments. Everywhere the prophets saw bad deeds, and kings and priests who allowed them. In the eighth century B.C., for example, the prophet Amos saw rich and powerful men trampling on the poor and defenseless. He saw crooked public officials living in luxury, while small farmers who could not pay their debts were sold into slavery. Yet, Amos said, the priests of the temple remained silent. Amos predicted disaster for the Hebrews unless they returned to God's ways.

"An enemy shall surround the land," Amos said. "Your sons and daughters shall fall by the sword. Hebrews shall be sent from their native land and go into exile." How could the people avoid such a fate? Amos told them, "Seek good, and not evil, that you may live."

The prophet Isaiah also warned the Hebrews that unless they obeyed the Ten Commandments, they would be punished. He saw the Assyrian soldiers as instruments of God's will. Isaiah claimed that God had said to him, "The Assyrian is the rod that I wield in my anger . . . . I send him against a godless nation. I bid him march against a people who rouse my wrath."

The Hebrews thus began to believe that God was not just *their* God. Rather, God's hand "stretched out over all nations" and over all people.

What did the ancient Hebrews and their prophets contribute to civilization? First, they held the idea of one, universal God and a religion based on moral ideals. Second, they insisted that religion must concern itself with social justice. Enemies would be "won over" not by military might, but by creating a fair society.

✎ Quick Check

1. *What were the two Hebrew kingdoms, and how many tribes did each have? What were their capitals?*

2. *What foreigners ruled over the two kingdoms after 853 B.C.? Which of the two kingdoms was destroyed first? Why was it destroyed? Who were "the 10 lost tribes of Israel"?*

3. *Was the surviving kingdom independent? Who was Nebuchadnezzar, and what did he do to the kingdom?*

4. *What puzzled the Hebrews about the destruction of their kingdoms by foreigners? What answers did their prophets give? What were the names of these prophets?*

PART 3
Review and Skills Exercises

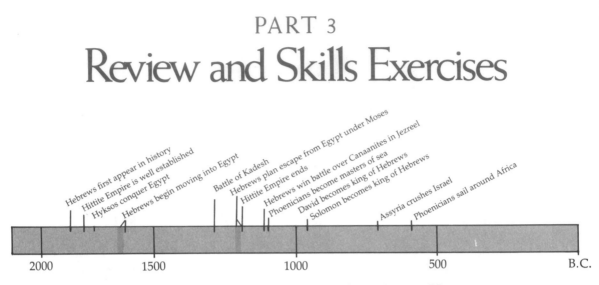

Timeline with events (left to right):
- Hebrews first appear in history
- Hittite Empire is well established
- Hyksos conquer Egypt
- Hebrews begin moving into Egypt
- Battle of Kadesh
- Hebrews plan escape from Egypt under Moses
- Hittite Empire ends
- Hebrews win battle over Canaanites in Jezreel
- Phoenicians become masters of sea
- David becomes king of Hebrews
- Solomon becomes king of Hebrews
- Assyria crushes Israel
- Phoenicians sail around Africa

Timeline scale: 2000 — 1500 — 1000 — 500 — B.C.

Understanding Events

Part 3 covers more than 1000 years of history, from the beginning of the Hittite Empire to the fall of the Hebrew kingdom of Judah. About the time that the Hittites were destroyed by the Philistines, the Phoenicians and the Hebrews were starting their rise to power in the Near East. Study the time line above and answer the following questions.

1. Around what time did the Hebrews begin moving into Egypt?

2. Approximately how many years were there between the Phoenicians becoming masters of the sea and their trip around Africa?

3. Which Hebrew king ruled closest to the present, David or Solomon?

4. Which event occurred first, the battle of Kadesh or the defeat of Israel by Assyria?

5. The Hyksos conquered Egypt around 1720 B.C. How many years ago was that from our own time?

Understanding a Source

You have read in Part 3 about some of the Hebrew prophets. The passage that follows is adapted from *A History of the Ancient World* by Chester G. Starr and tells more about these unusual people. Read the passage carefully and answer the questions below.

The ancient Near East had long known foretellers of the future. These were people who interpreted dreams, examined the livers of sheep, watched the flight of birds, or observed the stars. Generally such men were professionals and were organized in guilds. They handed down their secrets from father to son and usually worked for the kings. The prophets of Israel were of quite a different sort. They came from the common people and were driven by an urge to speak the word of God. They addressed the people as well as the monarch. Their prophecies were usually criticisms of the present rather than predictions of coming events.

The theme of almost all the prophets was the same. This theme was the covenant that linked God and his chosen people. The prophets advised people to obey God. If the people were proper in their service to God, said the prophets, God would protect them. If they were not proper and did such things as worship foreign gods, God would punish them. When the prophets saw the king or the rich oppressing the poor, for example, they cried out. They seemed to ignore the cost to themselves. The cost might be scorn or even physical punishment.

The messages of the prophets were usually unpleasant to hear. Sometimes they were hard to understand.

From the eighth century on, the words of the prophets were written down. Although their words were changed over the years, their views can still be found in the Bible. Across the ages the Hebrew prophets have appealed to many generations. They continue to appeal to people because they spoke of man's injustice to man.

1. According to the author, how were the Hebrew prophets different from other prophets of the Near East?

2. What was the message that almost all the prophets gave to the people?

3. Why do you think the messages of the prophets might have been "unpleasant to hear"? Why might people have disliked what the prophets said?

4. Where could you read the ideas of the Hebrew prophets today?

Building Vocabulary

On a separate sheet of paper, write the numbers 1-14. Read the words in column A. Then choose a definition from column B that best describes each word. Write the letter of your choice by each number on your paper.

A.

1. plundered
2. covenant
3. ethical
4. exodus
5. monarchy
6. monotheism
7. alliance
8. nomadic
9. peninsula
10. periodically
11. rebellion
12. Sabbath
13. treacherously
14. conquest

B.

a. the seventh day of the week

b. roaming from place to place

c. belief in one God

d. opposition to authority; uprising

e. victory, take over

f. conforming to certain standards of right and wrong

g. acting so as to betray a trust

h. rule by a single person such as a king

i. going out; mass departure

j. contract; agreement

k. portion of land nearly surrounded by water

l. occurring or recurring at certain intervals

m. an association for the common interests of the persons or groups involved, such as between two or more nations

n. taken by force, looted

PART
4

ANCIENT GREECE

"The world is full of wonders, but nothing is more wonderful than man."

A Greek writer proclaimed this in the fifth century B.C., when the civilization of ancient Greece was at its height. In one sentence, he summed up the most important beliefs of his countrymen. They were the following:

- Humans were special.
- They were worthy of honor and respect.
- They were worthy of being free and of ruling themselves.

Why were humans so wonderful? A Greek would have replied, "Only humans can build cities, create works of art, and develop sciences. They alone have the intelligence to guide their own lives and to know right from wrong."

Ideas like this were quite unusual in the world outside of Greece. In Egypt, Persia (now Iran), and other countries of the East, people still bowed down to god-kings. They never asked questions of their rulers, whose powers were absolute.

Such people, the Greeks said, were no better than slaves. Greeks, however, were free. They lived in small city-states, and in many of them the citizens ruled themselves. They were practicing *democracy*, a Greek word that means "rule by the people." In Greece, democratic government had its beginnings.

How did the world's first democracies compare with a modern democracy like our own? Even in the leading democratic city-state, Athens, many people could not take part in politics. About one third of the people were slaves. They were not citizens and had no political rights. Women could not vote or hold office. They were expected to devote themselves entirely to their husbands and children. Generally they were secluded in their homes.

That left only a minority of free male citizens to take part in government. Most of them, however, were small farmers who could not afford to leave their land for any length of time. So out of about 300,000 Athenians, including children, perhaps 10,000 were actively involved in the political system.

Athenians enjoyed the feeling that they, the people, made the decisions for their city-state. Aristotle (AR-ih-stah-tul), a great Greek philosopher who lived in the fourth century B.C., expressed his countrymen's viewpoint in the following words.

"Man is a political animal whose characteristic it is to live in a city-state."

The development of city-states in ancient Greece was influenced by the country's rugged terrain. Greece was divided by mountains, hills, and rivers into hundreds of separate areas. This led to the development of communities that were completely independent of each other. In early times, from about 1600 to 1200 B.C., they were ruled by kings. They developed a prosperous trade with the Egyptians, Hittites, Phoenicians, and others. With the wealth they gained, the kings built impressive palaces and strong defensive walls around their cities.

Brief Dark Age. But the walls weren't strong enough. Some time after 1200 B.C., a barbarian people known as the

The ancient Greeks valued human achievements. Below, scholars study in a Greek classroom. Page 104: A musician sings and strums a lyre.

107

Dorians swept into Greece from the north. The invaders destroyed everything in their path. Greek towns and their civilization lay in ruins. Trade ceased. For the next 300 years, the people survived by simple herding and farming.

This dark age ended around 800 B.C. when city-states once again arose in Greece. But now the kings were gone. Political power was in the hands of wealthy landowners who formed a class of nobles, or *aristocrats*. Gradually, over a period of many years, the power of the aristocrats was broken by the middle classes and the lower class of small farmers. In Athens, by the fifth century B.C., laws were passed by a system of direct democracy.

Fruits of Democracy. Under democratic governments, the city-states flourished as never before. Greeks were very proud of themselves. In their view, the human race was made up of two kinds of people. First there were those who spoke Greek. Then there were all the others who did not speak Greek. These "unfortunates" were called barbarians. This did not mean people who lived in caves and wore animal skins. Even people who lived luxuriously in Egypt, or Persia were considered barbarians.

The Greeks, in fact, had much to be proud of. They were the first people to write plays and act in them. Many of their plays are still performed today. They were also the first to write history. They created or perfected mathematics and many of the natural sciences. They

produced the first philosophers and the first great poets. The creative genius of the ancient Greeks still dazzles us in the twentieth century.

Greek society owed many debts to a culture that developed on the nearby island of Crete beginning around 2800 B.C. The people who developed this culture, called Minoans, were very skilled in the arts. They were also successful farmers and merchants. We shall look more closely at this civilization in Chapter 15.

The greatest loyalty of the ancient Greeks was to their city-states. Only there, they believed, could civilized life be so fulfilling. They were certain that there was no better way to live.

What happened to the Greek city-states? Rivalry between the strongest of them, Athens and Sparta, led to all-out war in 431 B.C. Both had many allies among the other city-states. The war dragged on for 27 terrible years. Sparta finally defeated Athens, but it was a hollow victory. The war left all the city-states exhausted and demoralized. They were easily conquered by a kingdom in the north called Macedonia. A young Macedonian king who became known as Alexander the Great united the city-states by force.

Alexander had always admired the Greeks. As a youth, his teacher was the philosopher Aristotle. Alexander went on to conquer half the known world and create a huge empire. In the great cities of this empire, Greek learning and culture prevailed.

ANCIENT GREECE (ABOUT 450 B.C.)

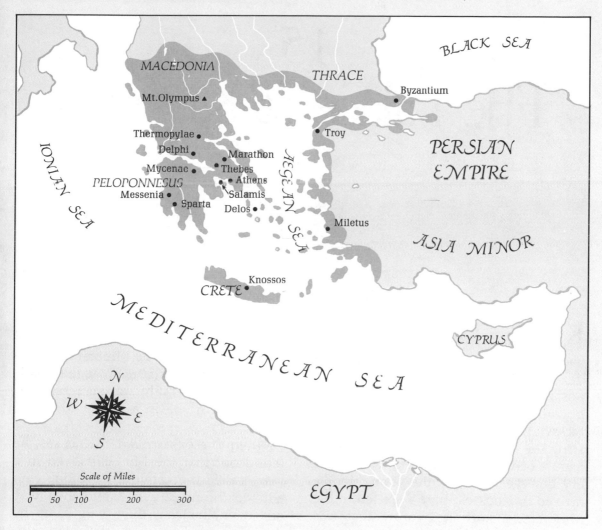

MAP EXERCISE

This map shows many of the cities of ancient Greece. Use it to answer the following:

1. What empire lay to the east of the Greek city-states? What land lay to the north?

2. Imagine you are in ancient Athens. How far would you have to travel to reach Sparta? To reach Knossos?

3. Which Greek city was located on a peninsula between the Black Sea and the Aegean?

4. How far was it from Athens to the delta of the Nile?

15
The Palace at Knossos

King Aegeus (EE-gee-us) of Athens had a great problem. He had caused the death of the son of Minos (MY-nos). Minos was king of Knossos (NAW-suss), a powerful city in Crete. Furious, Minos attacked Athens. He said that he would destroy the city unless Aegeus sent him a tribute of 14 young men and women every nine years. When the young people arrived in Knossos, they were fed to the Minotaur, a horrible creature that was half-man and half-bull.

Theseus (THEE-see-uss) was Aegeus's son. Through a trick of fate, Theseus did not meet his father until he was a young man. He was already famed for his brave, good deeds. He met his father just when the young men and women were being chosen for the tribute. Against his father's wishes, Theseus volunteered to

join the unfortunate youths. He swore that he would kill the Minotaur and return to Athens unharmed. Aegeus made him promise that if he was successful, he would sail home in a ship with white sails.

When Theseus arrived in Knossos, he found out that the Minotaur lived in a maze called the Labyrinth. No one who entered the maze ever found their way out again. Instead, they were eaten by the Minotaur. Fortunately, a Cretan princess called Ariadne (ah-ree-AHD-nee) fell in love with Theseus. She showed him how he could find his way out of the Labyrinth. She gave him a ball of thread and stood holding one end of it at the entrance to the maze. Theseus unwound the thread behind him as he walked through the maze. When he found the

According to myth, Theseus of Athens (left, carrying a queen out of battle) sailed to the island of Crete and killed the Minotaur, a half-man, half-bull that lived in a maze called the Labyrinth. This freed Athenians from having to sacrifice young men and women to the horrible monster each year.

Minotaur, he killed it with his bare hands. Using the thread, he retraced his steps to find his way out. He then escaped from Knossos with Ariadne. However, she was not rewarded for her help. Theseus deserted her on the island of Naxos.

Unfortunately, he forgot his promise to his father. He sailed into Athens on a ship with black sails. Thinking that Theseus was dead, Aegeus leaped into the sea from a high cliff. Theseus then became king of Athens.

Through the ages Cretan peasants have believed that their island was the center of a powerful people hundreds of years before Athens became a great city. They based their beliefs on the ancient *myth*, or story, of Theseus. Others have scoffed at these beliefs.

Evans Finds Proof. Not until the beginning of this century was it revealed that the myth was grounded in truth. An Englishman named Arthur Evans organized a dig at what was said to be the site of Knossos. There he found the ruins of a palace that had been destroyed hundreds of years before the age of classical Greece. He called the people of this civilization Minoans (MIN-oh-enz) after the legendary king Minos. Their civilization lasted from about 2800 B.C. to 712 B.C. Other digs on Crete have unearthed other cities and palaces, all built by Minoans.

The Minoans were a very skilled people for their time. The palace at Knossos covered six acres, with a surrouding

town of 22 acres. Its population has been estimated at 100,000. The largest city in Crete today has only a third as many people. The palace at Knossos was built in a complicated arrangement of rooms. It even had a plumbing system with indoor toilets. Its walls were decorated with colored paintings called *frescoes* (FRESS-koez). The palace and town of Knossos were protected by a powerful and well-equipped navy.

The Minoans had a written language known today as Linear A script. But historians have not yet learned to read it. Most of our knowledge of the Minoans comes from the frescoes. They show the Minoans at work and at play.

Apparently they were good farmers. Probably Crete had a more fertile soil than it does today. The palace had dozens of enormous jars that held olive oil, honey, grain, and other crop surpluses. With abundant food, the Minoans had plenty of time to devote to making useful and beautiful objects. Their pottery and metalwork were the finest the world had ever seen. They also spent much time making clothing and ornaments. Women wore elaborate gowns with many petticoats and complex embroidery. Both men and women wore jewelry.

Besides a navy, the Minoans had a strong merchant fleet. The boats were built for long voyages. They were driven with both oars and sails. The Minoan merchants traded their crops and crafts with other people, especially the Egyptians and Syrians. In return they got gold

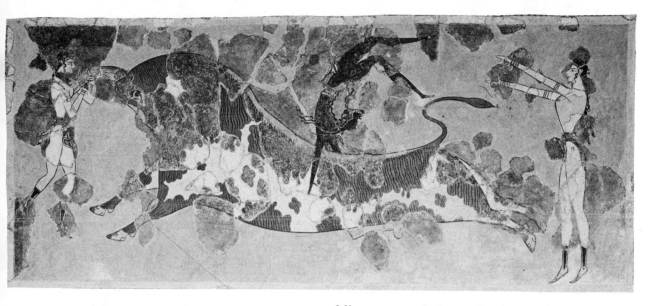

Minoan women had many freedoms and participated in sports like bull-leaping (above). A fragment of a fresco (left) shows how they dressed.

and other minerals that could not be found on the island.

The Minoans enjoyed sports, especially boxing and an activity one might call bull-leaping. Teams of young men and women would perform acrobatics with charging bulls. They would grasp the bulls' horns and backflip over them into each other's arms. This sport was very dangerous. Modern-day rodeo experts say that it would be impossible to do without seriously risking one's life.

Independent Women. In the frescoes, Minoan women are shown to have many freedoms that were denied to women in some other ancient cultures. They attended athletic events, both as players and spectators. They went hunting and to the theater.

113

Why were Minoan women so free? Possibly because the main deity of the Minoans was the Mother Goddess. She was believed to be the mother of all people. She also made plants grow and bear fruit. Another one of her names was Snake Goddess. Snakes were fed and housed in every household and worshipped as guardians of the home. It was believed that women who were blessed by the goddess were permitted to bear children. Thus women had special status, especially after they became mothers. Some historians believe that the queens of Knossos were worshipped as representatives of the Goddess.

What historical basis is there for the myth of Theseus and the Minotaur? It is certainly possible that a Minoan king forced Athens to send young men and women to Crete as tribute. Instead of becoming food for a monster, the youths may have been trained as bull-leapers. Considering the danger of that sport, it would have been unlikely for anyone to survive for long.

By 712 B.C., Minoan civilization had practically disappeared. Why? To begin with, Crete is located in an area where natural disasters are common. There was a major volcanic eruption on the island of Thera (THEER-uh) around 1520 B.C. Thera is 60 miles north of Crete. The eruption was so great that it caused huge tidal waves and earthquakes that destroyed Cretan lives and buildings. In addition, volcanic ash covered the fields. This made it impossible to grow crops.

Already weakened by natural disasters, the Minoans were easy prey to Greek invaders from the north. Most of the invaders were Mycenean (my-SEE-nee-an) Greeks. These Greeks were rough and crude compared to the Minoans. They overthrew the government of Knossos and destroyed the palace in the fourteenth century B.C. Probably they often lost their way in the confusing corridors, rooms, and courtyards of the palace. This might have accounted for the story of the Labyrinth.

Under Greek rule, Minoan culture endured for many more centuries. Its agriculture, religion, art, and architecture greatly influenced the Myceneans. The Myceneans were the ancestors of the people who brought Greek civilization to its height many centuries later. Thus, the Minoans passed on a sophisticated culture that paved the way for the glories of classical Greece.

✎ **Quick Check**

1. *According to the myth, what was the Minotaur, and where did it live? Who finally killed it, and how did he escape?*

2. *Who discovered the ruins of the Minoans? When did they thrive? Briefly describe the palace at Knossos, the livelihood of the people, and their entertainment.*

3. *How were Minoan women different from those of other ancient cultures? What is one possible explanation for this?*

4. *What might explain the disappearance of the Minoans? Who invaded Crete? When? What happened to Minoan culture?*

16
The Myths of Greece

The early Greeks worshipped many gods and goddesses. Many myths were told about them. Some explained natural occurrences, such as why and how the sun rose every morning. Typically, a deity was responsible for this. But the early Greeks did not want deities who were perfect and had complete power over the lives of human beings, or *mortals*. Instead, their deities had human failings and weaknesses, and often lost their self-control.

People believed that the deities looked like humans, only more perfect. And they made mistakes so that people could learn from them and avoid making the same mistakes. Although it was a terrible crime to think oneself greater than the gods and goddesses, people considered themselves almost equal to them. Greeks could even bargain with their deities. If a man sacrificed a sheep to a goddess, he expected the goddess to do something for him in return.

It was believed that most of the gods and goddesses lived on Mount Olympus, a mountain in Greece. They kept themselves immortal by eating ambrosia (am-BRO-shuh) and drinking nectar (NEK-ter), which only they knew how to make.

Zeus (zooce) was the most powerful of the gods. He was believed to be the father of all Greeks. He could kill any person who angered him with a thunderbolt. But even Zeus had weaknesses. He loved women and often lied to his wife, the goddess Hera (HEH-rah). She was worshipped as the goddess of the home, but she was often cruel and unjust. She was a jealous wife and tried to punish the women that Zeus loved. Zeus's brothers Poseidon (po-SIDE-un) and Hades (HAY-deez) controlled the sea and the underworld, where the dead lived. Athena (a-THEE-neh), Zeus's daughter, was a powerful goddess who represented reason, virtue, and purity. Myth has it that she was not born of a goddess, but sprang from Zeus's forehead, adult and in full armor.

Athena (left), guardian of Athens, was goddess of wisdom. Greek mythology holds she was born from the head of Zeus dressed for battle.

Apollo (uh-PAH-loh) controlled the sun and helped humans to understand the deities and get along with them. His sister Artemis (ar-TEM-iss) controlled the moon and was worshipped as the goddess of the hunt. Aphrodite (aff-ro-DYE-tee) was the goddess of love and beauty. Her son Eros (EH-roce) could make both deities and humans fall in love by shooting them with his golden arrows. Demeter (dee-MEE-ter) was the goddess who controlled all growing things. People prayed to her for a good harvest. These were only some of the dozens of deities that the Greeks worshipped.

Sometimes, it was thought, a person could become immortal if they were loved by a god or goddess. The following myth "Eros and Psyche," is a good example of this idea.

Psyche (SY-kee) was a human woman who was so beautiful that people had started to worship her instead of Aphrodite. Aphrodite was furious at her because of this. She told her son, Eros, to make Psyche fall in love with a horrible monster. Eros tried to obey, but when he saw Psyche, he fell in love with her himself. He arranged to have her brought to a beautiful palace. There, he secretly married her and visited her only in the dark, so that she could not see him and find out that he was a god. He told her that she must never try to look at him. Even without seeing him, Psyche fell in love with him.

Eventually, Psyche became lonely and, against Eros's wishes, invited her sisters to visit her. When they found out that she had never seen her husband, they were horrified. They persuaded her that he might be a monster. Against her better instincts, Psyche shone a lamp on her husband one night. She was prepared to cut off his head if he really was a monster. Instead, she saw that he was Eros, young, handsome, with golden wings. Suddenly, Eros woke up and saw his wife standing over him with a knife. Full of sorrow, he flew out the window and back to Mount Olympus.

Psyche was determined to get her husband to return to her. She prayed to Demeter for guidance. Demeter advised her to serve Aphrodite. By now Aphrodite hated Psyche even more for stealing her son's love. She ordered Psyche to perform various tasks, each more impossible than the last. Eros secretly helped her to perform them. He wanted to return to Psyche, but he was afraid of his mother. Finally, Aphrodite gave Psyche her most impossible task. She told her to go to the underworld and get a box of beauty from the queen of the dead. With the help of Demeter, Psyche managed to get the box of beauty and leave the underworld. On her way to Aphrodite, she opened the box in order to steal a little of the beauty. Clouds of dark mist came out of the box and put her in a death-like sleep.

Eros woke Psyche up and realized that he had to help her make peace with his mother. He went to Zeus and begged him to make Psyche immortal so that she would be on an equal footing with the deities. Zeus obliged and had Psyche brought up to Mount Olympus. He gave Psyche ambrosia and nectar, and she became immortal. Aphrodite had to relent when her daughter-in-law became her equal. She forgave Psyche, and the couple lived happily together on Mount Olympus.

A More Sympathetic Faith. What does this myth show about the Greek deities? Mainly, it shows that they could be reached, and their motives were easily understood. The very idea that a human can become immortal makes the Greek religion different from the other religions of its time. While other peoples lived in fear of cruel, distant, and puzzling deities, the Greeks were fearless. Although they believed in an afterlife, the spirits of the dead were pitied, rather than feared. As Psyche shows, a person could go to the underworld and survive without harm. There were no evil spirits in the woods, but lovely nymphs and mischievous half-man, half-horse creatures called centaurs. The only mystery was in the future. While it was believed that the deities could control the fates of humans, they usually did not bother. A person had to be unusual for the deities to decide his or her fate.

The Greek deities are important characters in early Greek poems and plays. Homer, the earliest known Greek poet, blamed three goddesses for a major war between Greece and Troy. In his *Iliad* (ILL-ee-ahd), a young Trojan man, Paris, was asked to choose which of three goddesses was the most beautiful. To bribe him, Hera offered him great wealth. Athena offered him great victory in war. Aphrodite offered him the love of Helen, the most beautiful woman in the world. Paris accepted Aphrodite's offer. The problem was that Helen was already married to a Greek king. When Paris stole Helen away to Troy, the Greeks decided to go to war against the Trojans. The war lasted 10 years and claimed the lives of some of the best and bravest warriors on both sides. According to Homer, the Greeks won because most of the deities were on their side.

Until the nineteenth century, it was believed that Troy was a mythical place.

Athena inspects the Trojan Horse (above). Legend says unsuspecting Trojans wheeled the huge wooden horse into Troy. Armed Greeks were hidden in its belly.

Then a German archaeologist set out to find it. He discovered the ruins of a city in northwestern Asia Minor that had been destroyed by Greek invaders.

No one knows for sure whether the Trojan war actually occurred. The important thing was that the Greeks believed it. They respected the deities that had helped them to victory. As in the myths, the deities of Homer make mistakes. They are jolly and sometimes comical. However, they are also powerful and therefore worthy of respect.

The Power of the Deities. After Homer's time, the Greeks began to weave their myths and poems into plays. Aeschylus (ESS-kyuh-luss) was the earliest known playwright. He wrote tragedies. In them, noble or powerful characters clashed with destiny and came to unhappy ends. In all these plays, the deities had great power. Usually, they punished anyone who committed crimes against them or humans. For example, if a son killed his mother, he was severely punished, no matter what the circumstances.

However, as time wore on, Greeks began to question the old images of the gods and goddesses. The old deities only understood the simplest forms of justice. As Greece became organized into city-states, people began to think about justice. As life got more complicated, so did the responses of the Greek deities.

The playwright Euripides (you-RIP-uh-deez) was one of the first to believe that the deities were always just. He wrote, "Do not say that those in heaven are corrupt. For a long time I have known that this is false."

Euripides believed that the deities did not interfere directly with human lives, but rather inspired people to behave justly. But he knew that the divine wisdom was sometimes lost on humans. In his tragedy *The Trojan Women*, the deities cannot help the victims, because the oppressors do not understand true justice.

Euripides was unpopular in his own time. But after his death, people began to read his plays and understand what he had been trying to say.

✎ Quick Check

1. *Where did the Greek deities live, and how did they become immortal? Who was the most powerful god? Who were members of his family? Name three other deities, and what they represented.*

2. *Who was Psyche? Why was Aphrodite jealous of her? Who married her? What eventually happened to her?*

3. *How were the Greek deities different from the deities of other peoples at that time?*

4. *What is the* Iliad? *Who wrote it? According to the* Iliad, *what caused the Trojan war? Who won? Did this war actually occur in history?*

5. *Who was Aeschylus? What did he believe about the deities? Who was Euripides? How were his beliefs different from Aeschylus's?*

17
Athens: The Spirit of Learning

Greece had hundreds of city-states, but two became stronger and greater than the others. They were Athens and Sparta. These city-states had very different ways of life. Athens became a great democracy, ruled by its free men. Sparta became a soldier-state, ruled by a small group of men. The wealth of Athens came from its trade and colonies. Sparta's wealth came from land worked by slaves. In this chapter and the next we shall learn more about life in these two places.

The year: about 450 B.C.

The place: a busy street in Athens.

The action: two citizens, Ariston (AH-ruh-ston) and Cleros (KLAIR-ohz), are walking to the marketplace.

ARISTON: It looks like another fine sunny day, Cleros. There's not a cloud in the sky. And the sea breeze is as cool as ever.

CLEROS: What did you expect, Ariston? Who but the Greeks are blessed with such a climate? It keeps us outdoors and makes us healthy too.

(Suddenly a boy throws a pail of garbage into the street, shouting, "Out of the way.")

ARISTON: That fool slave boy! Why doesn't he watch where he throws the garbage? He almost hit me!

CLEROS: He's just a slave. Don't expect him to have any sense.

ARISTON: Say, it's getting crowded. The marketplace will be busier than ever today. If only people wouldn't push and shove!

CLEROS: If you want to enjoy city life, Ariston, you have to put up with such things.

(The two men enter the marketplace. It is a large, open square filled with wooden booths. From these booths, merchants shout, "Fresh bread for sale!" "Buy fish!" "Olive oil today! Get it today! Get it cheap!" Around the square are long, covered walks and temples to the gods and goddesses.)

ARISTON: Cleros, do you see what I see? Isn't that the wife of Paros (PAH-roz) buying flowers?

CLEROS: Shocking! No decent woman should be seen in public! And here, among the rabble of the marketplace! She must have sneaked out of her house. Wait until Paros hears about this!

(A group of men are talking about the news of the day. Ariston stops to listen to them for a while. Then he rejoins Cleros.)

The artwork on this Greek urn shows women gathering apples in an orchard.

CLEROS: What are they saying?

ARISTON: Good news! Our fleet has won a great victory over the Persians at Cyprus (SY-press)! Perhaps now the king of Persia will leave our colonies in Asia alone. When will he learn that Persians can never defeat free Greeks?

CLEROS: Persians are slow to learn, Ariston. That is why we must keep our fleet strong at all times.

ARISTON: By the way, Cleros, is it true what people are saying about our noble leader, Pericles (PEH-ruh-cleez)? Does he really want to *pay* citizens to serve on juries?

CLEROS: Why, yes, Ariston. Does that bother you?

ARISTON: Really, Cleros, you surprise me. You know as well as I do that a man's first duty is to serve his city. The highest reward that any man could want is to take part in his government. Why should anyone have to be paid for it?

CLEROS: Let's be practical, Ariston. How many men can afford to leave their jobs or farms to serve the city? We have about 30,000 citizens in Athens. Every one of them is supposed to vote on new laws. Yet how many of them actually do vote in the assembly? Usually no more than 6,000. And the reason for it is that most citizens can't afford the time to go to meetings. I think Pericles has the right idea. If we pay our citizens to take part in running the government, more will be able to serve. It will make Athens even more democratic than it is now.

Among the ancient Greeks were the world's first playwrights. This stone carving depicts a scene from a Greek comedy.

ARISTON: Perhaps you are right, Cleros. I never thought of it that way. Say, what are you doing this afternoon?

CLEROS: I think I'll go to my gymnasium, Ariston. A man must have a healthy body as well as an educated mind. Besides, I hear Euripides (you-RIP-uh-deez) will be there. He's written a play, and I want to know about it.

ARISTON: I would like to meet this new writer. Do you mind if I come along with you?

CLEROS: Not at all. See you at the gym after lunch.

✎ Quick Check

1. *What two city-states of Greece became stronger than the others? How were they different from one another?*

2. *Who was allowed to take part in the government of Athens? Who was not? How many citizens were there? How many actually voted?*

3. *What did the Athenians think of the people from lands outside of Greece?*

4. *Why did Ariston think people should not be paid for serving on juries? Why did Cleros think they should?*

18
Sparta: Home of the Brave

Stranger, tell the Spartans that we lie here obedient to their laws."

These words were written on the grave of 300 Spartan soldiers. They had fought to the last man against a large army of Persians at Thermopylae (thur-MAHP-eh-lee) in 480 B.C. Before the battle, they were told that the arrows of the Persians would fly in such numbers that they would hide the sun. A Spartan soldier said, "So much the better. We shall fight in the shade."

Spartan soldiers were the best in Greece, and they were very brave. They did not give up or run. They fought until they won—or died. Spartan fighters were trained to be that way from the time they were born. They were taught to become good soldiers and obey their leaders. They were not allowed to have any trade or job. That was for slaves. Spartan men had to be soldiers, and nothing else.

Why did Sparta raise its boys to become professional soldiers? Like other Greek city-states, Sparta did not have enough land to feed its people. Other city-states solved the problem by sending some of their people to overseas colonies. Sparta solved the problem another way. It made war on its neighbor, Messenia (meh-SEE-nee-uh). Sparta took over the land of Messenia and made slaves of the people. In the area Sparta now ruled, there were about 10 slaves for every Spartan citizen.

About 650 B.C., the slaves rebelled against their masters. It took the Spartans almost 20 years to put down the

slaves. After that the Spartans lived in fear of other slave rebellions. They decided that they should have a strong army ready at all times. So Spartans were trained to be tough soldiers and obey orders. They spent almost all their time building their bodies. They cared very little about improving their minds. Usually they looked down upon any new ideas.

Athletic Women. Spartan women lived very differently from those of Athens. They were citizens and were considered the equals of men. Although they could not become soldiers, they were strong and athletic. Young girls did not do housework or sew like Athenian girls did. That sort of work was considered only fit for slaves. Instead, girls wrestled, boxed, raced, and generally lived an outdoor life. The state encouraged this. It was believed that athletic women would have healthy sons who would become good soldiers. Women married when they were about 20 years old. They were encouraged to have as many children as possible. Sometimes women had two husbands at once and had children with both of them.

Family life was controlled by the state. Husbands and wives did not spend much time together. Husbands were usually off at war, or training with their fellow soldiers. Plutarch (PLOO-tark), a Greek historian, noted that sometimes married couples spent only a little time together in the evenings. Sometimes they were married for months before they saw each other in the daylight. Daughters were raised at home, but not sons. Young boys were taken from their parents and trained as future soldiers.

Training of Agis. Agis (AY-jess) was a typical Spartan boy. Soon after he was born, a group of Spartan leaders looked him over. They saw that he was a healthy baby and gave him back to his parents. Agis was lucky. Sick or weak Spartan babies were thrown into a deep hole to die.

Agis had parents who did not spoil him. They taught him to be content with very plain food. They taught him not to fear the dark and never to cry.

At the age of seven, Agis had to leave home and live in a camp with other young boys. He slept on a hard bed and wore few clothes, even in cold weather. He was taught by a trainer

- to stand pain,
- to speak only when he was spoken to,
- to answer in a few words,
- to respect his elders without question,
- to obey every order completely,
- to harden his body, and
- to eat very little.

When Agis became a teenager, he was sometimes sent to live alone in the woods. He was given no food. He had to find food, or steal it. If he didn't, he would starve. If caught, he would be whipped. This was to train the future soldier to take care of himself.

Agis and the other boys in his camp played rough games. In one game, two teams of 15 players each fought each other to keep a ball. Biting, punching, and kicking were allowed. The winning team was the one that had the ball when time was called. In another game, two teams fought each other on an island in a river. The team that pushed the other into the river won.

Spartan sports were not always so rough. Agis was taught to drill and exercise with music playing. He and the other boys were taught to read and write. But they had very little use for books.

At 18, Agis was considered a man. He trained with the army and was allowed to let his hair grow long. Spartans believed that long hair was a sign of manliness. They liked to curl it and adorn it too. At 24, Agis became a first-class soldier. At 30, he became a full citizen. He was now allowed to marry and start a family. It was the first time he lived in a real home since he was a small boy.

Even so, Agis had to eat dinner every day with other soldiers rather than with his family. He often slept in the soldiers' barracks, rather than at home. When war came, he had to put on his armor and march off. He had to serve in the army until he was 60.

It was better for Agis not to run away or give up in a battle. The Spartans were rough on "cowards." Soldiers who quit in a battle lost all their rights. Other Spartans would have nothing to do with them or with their families. Spartan women had the same spirit. When a Spartan soldier went to war, his mother told him, "Come back with your shield, or on it."

✎ Quick Check

1. *What occupations could Spartan men choose?*

2. *How did Sparta get so many slaves? What problem did this cause? How did Spartans respond to this problem?*

3. *How were the lives of Spartan women different from Athenian women? Describe Spartan homelife?*

4. *How old was Agis when he left home? How was he taught to react to pain? To orders? To hunger?*

5. *How did the Spartans treat soldiers they considered cowards?*

19
Heroes of Marathon

King Darius (duh-RYE-us) of Persia wanted to punish Athens. He knew how to do it. He would burn the city to the ground and make slaves of its people. Then he would send them away to a distant part of his vast empire.

Why was Darius so angry with Athens? The king of Persia was a proud man. He was the master of a great empire that reached from India to Egypt. In this empire, everyone had to bow to the "Great King." They had to pay him tribute and provide soldiers to serve in his armies. They were ruled by his governors.

But in 499 B.C., Greek colonies in Asia Minor rebelled against Persian rule. They asked Athens to help. Athens sent 20 warships to Asia Minor. These ships helped the rebels burn a Persian city. Later the Persians put down the rebellion, but Darius never forgave Athens for aiding it.

Battle at Marathon. In 492 B.C., Darius sent a large fleet with soldiers to punish Athens. He now meant to add all of Greece to his empire. This fleet was wrecked at sea by a storm. But two years later Darius sent another fleet of 600 ships to Athens. This time the fleet put the Persian army ashore at Marathon, only 26 miles from Athens. There the Persian army of about 25,000 men set up camp.

The citizens of Athens voted to send an army to Marathon at once. About 10,000 men were able to answer the call to arms. They went home, put on their armor, took their weapons, and marched off. The Athenian army set up camp on a mountain one mile from the Persians.

Now the 10 generals of Athens wondered what to do. They could see that the Persian army was much larger than their own. The Persians also had mounted sol-

127

diers and men with bows and arrows. The Athenians had neither. Some of the Athenian generals were against attacking the Persians. It would be safer to stay where they were. Besides, the Spartans had promised to send help in a few days. It would be better to wait for the Spartans to arrive before fighting the Persians.

Other generals wanted to attack the Persians quickly. One of them, Miltiades (mil-TIE-ah-deez), had good reasons: He feared that traitors inside Athens might try to make a deal with the Persians. He believed that free Greek citizens fighting for their homes could defeat the Persian "slaves."

The generals finally agreed to support Miltiades. He became the leader of the Athenian army. Miltiades ordered the Athenians to attack on the run. He wanted to close the space between the two armies quickly. He believed that in close fighting the Greeks would have many advantages. The Greeks wore body armor; the Persians did not. Greek shields were made of metal and hides; Persian shields were made of twigs. Greek spears were longer than Persian spears.

The Persians were amazed when they saw the Athenians running toward them. They thought the Athenians were madmen, rushing to get killed.

Soon the Greek weapons and style of fighting were too much for the Persians. Early in the battle the Persians broke through the center of the Greek line. But the two ends of the Greek line wheeled around and formed a line behind the Persians. The Persians fought bravely. But solid rows of Greek shields and long spears were too much for them. Finally, the Persians ran back to their ships. The Greeks chased them and captured seven of their ships. The rest of the Persian fleet put to sea.

Miltiades sent a runner to Athens with news of the victory. This was the first *marathon* (a race of the same distance covered by Miltiades' runner). But the Persian commander had a trick up his sleeve. He ordered his fleet to sail to Athens. He hoped the city would be without guards to defend it. Then traitors might turn the city over to him. But Miltiades guessed the Persian commander's plan. He marched most of his army overland to Athens. When the Persian fleet arrived, its commander could see the Athenian soldiers ready and waiting. The Persians knew their cause was hopeless. They sailed back to Asia.

The next day a Spartan army arrived at Marathon. The army saw the dead on the battlefield. There were 6,400 Persians and 192 Athenians. The Athenian heroes were buried in a mound that can still be seen today.

Persian Defeat Leads to Golden Age. The Athenian victory at Marathon did not stop the Persians from attacking Greece again. But it did show the other city-states that the Persians could be beaten. It gave some Greeks the will to resist and even to unite against the Persians. In 480 B.C., the Greeks united against the next Persian attack. The Persian army defeated a small Spartan army at Thermopylae. Every Spartan was killed defending the mountain pass. Then the Persians took Athens and burned its temples.

But soon after, the Greek fleet almost wiped out a larger Persian fleet. This crushing defeat forced most of the Persian army to go home. The rest of the Persians were driven from Greece for good the next year. It meant that freedom and the worth of man would not die.

The defeat of the Persians filled all Greeks with pride especially Athenians. They would never forget their heroes. The Athenians gained great confidence in their own abilities. A "Golden Age" was about to begin for Athens in politics, trade, the arts, and sciences.

✎ Quick Check

1. *Who was Darius? How large was his empire? What was his attitude toward the Greeks? Why?*

2. *Where did the major Persian-Greek battle take place? When? Who led the Greeks? What did he believe? What was his military plan?*

3. *Why were the Greeks considered heroes for winning this battle? Why was a runner sent to Athens?*

4. *Who fought at Thermopylae? Who won? What were the consequences?*

At Marathon, the Athenians fought powerful King Darius of Persia (seated).

PERSIA VERSUS GREECE

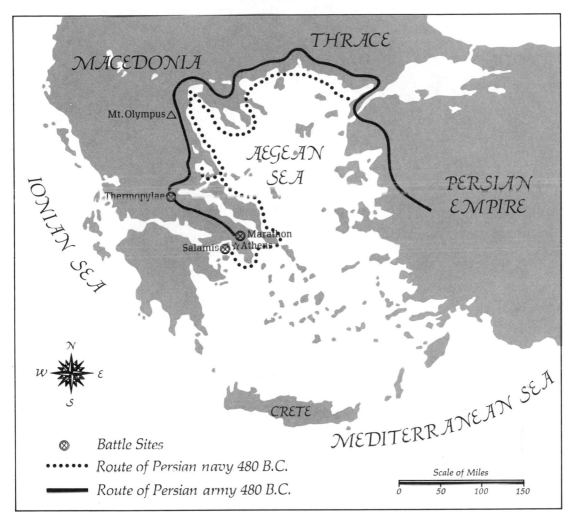

MAP EXERCISE

The Persian army and navy both tried to overpower the Greeks. Use the map to answer the following questions:

1. How far across the sea was the Persian Empire from Athens?

2. What body of water is located to the west of the Greek city-states?

3. Which sea did the Persian navy sail through to reach Salamis?

20
The Golden Age

Athens was the liveliest city in all of Greece. People rushed to see great plays in large outdoor theaters. On a high hill called the Acropolis, new temples and statues of the gods and goddesses were built. In busy streets, men argued about the meaning of justice, truth, and goodness. In gymnasiums they boxed, wrestled, and trained their bodies. Thousands of them met almost every week to hear their leaders and make new laws.

It was the Golden Age of Athens. It began about 479 B.C. after the defeat of the Persians. Athens was then the richest and strongest Greek city-state. Its great wealth gave many men free time to serve their city and enjoy the good life.

How did Athens become so rich and strong? No one had done more than the Athenians to save Greece from the Persians. When the Persians were defeated, Athens had a very powerful navy. Now Athens asked other Greek city-states to join it in a league.

Athens offered to protect them against the Persians. They, in return, would pay Athens either in ships or money. Many city-states thought this was a good idea and joined the league. Athens grew rich and powerful as its leader.

The Athenians built temples supported by graceful columns (right) on a high hill called the Acropolis.

Wisest Man in Athens. During its Golden Age, Athens had many great writers, artists, and wise men. The wisest of all was a short, fat, homely man who was too poor to buy shoes. His name was Socrates (SOCK-rah-teez). Everyone in Athens knew him.

He could always be found, either in the streets, the marketplace, or a gym. And he was always talking. Mostly he liked to ask questions, lots of questions. What, he asked, was the meaning of truth? Of goodness? Of right or wrong? Of justice? His questions often made people angry.

Socrates wanted Athenians to think for themselves. He wanted them to look for the truth and not accept what other people *said* was true.

Socrates asked many questions, but he rarely gave answers. He believed that the wisest people were those who admitted that they knew very little. Only the deities were really wise. People who boasted that they were wise were just fools.

Socrates loved to show these "wise" men how foolish they were. He would ask them questions that seemed very simple at first. But soon he would set a trap for them. Then their answers would become nonsense, and they would feel very stupid. This is how Socrates would question a man who thought he was very wise:

SOCRATES: Tell me, if you can, what is courage?

MAN: Easy. A man has courage if he fights against the enemy and does not run away.

SOCRATES: Very well. Then courage is something very noble. Is that true?

MAN: Very true.

SOCRATES: Suppose a man does not run away when the enemy is sure to kill him. What would you call that?

MAN: I would call that very foolish.

SOCRATES: But isn't it also courage?

MAN: Well...I suppose so.

SOCRATES: Then you are saying that courage is both noble and foolish? How can that be?

MAN: I don't know. You've got me all mixed up. I don't know what I'm saying anymore.

Death of Socrates. During its Golden Age, Athens respected a man like Socrates. Even though his questions disturbed people, most agreed he was the wisest man among them. But the Golden Age ended after Athens went to war with Sparta. Hard times and disorder came to the city. Many people then believed that Socrates was a dangerous troublemaker. Because of him, they said, men were not loyal to the city or the deities. Socrates was put on trial for "not worshipping the deities and for corrupting the young men of the city."

Socrates refused to save his life by saying he was wrong and asking for mercy. Instead he boldly defended himself. His only crime, he said, was searching for

The Greek philosopher Socrates died as he lived, asking questions in the search for truth. This famous eighteenth-century painting by Jacques Louis David shows Socrates on his deathbed.

truth and wisdom. The deities themselves had commanded him to do so, he told the jury.

Socrates was found guilty. He was sentenced to death by drinking poison. His friends were with him in jail. He advised them to follow the path of life pointed out in the conversations they had together. Then he calmly drank the cup of poisonous hemlock. Until the very end, he asked them questions.

✎ Quick Check

1. *What was the purpose of the league of Greek city-states? Which city-state headed it? Why?*

2. *Describe Athens in its Golden Age. When did it begin? What marked its end?*

3. *Who was Socrates? How did he live? What did he believe?*

4. *How did the Athenians' feelings about Socrates change? Why? What finally happened to him?*

135

21
The Olympic Games

The place: Olympia, Greece.

The year: 212 B.C.

The event: a championship boxing match.

The Greek boxer was annoyed. The large crowd of spectators was rooting for his opponent, an Egyptian. Why, he wondered, should Greeks watching an Olympic contest cheer for a foreigner? Yet it was true. Each time the Egyptian, Aristonicus (ar-ih-STON-ih-cuss), landed a punch, there was a burst of applause. The crowd would shout, "Keep up your courage, Aristonicus!" They wanted him to win because he was the underdog against Clitomachus (klee-TOE-mack-us), who was a champion. Finally the Greek boxer, Clitomachus, turned to the spectators and spoke.

"Have I committed a foul or broken the rules?" he asked. "Do you not know that I am fighting for the glory of Greece? Aristonicus fights for the glory of King Ptolemy (TAHL-eh-mee) of Egypt. Would you prefer an Egyptian to carry off the Olympic championship by beating Greeks?"

These words swayed the spectators. They began to root for Clitomachus, who went on to win the fight. An ancient historian wrote about this boxing match. He said that the Egyptian was beaten "more by the temper of the crowd than by Clitomachus."

When this boxing match took place, the Olympic Games were already more than five centuries old. Modern historians say that the Olympics began in 776 B.C. That was the year the first official list of winners was kept. But the Olympic Games were held even before that. They lasted well over 1000 years, until 394 A.D. At that time, the Roman emperor, Theo-

dosius, (thee-oh-DOE-shuss) put an end to them. He said they went against the spirit of Christianity. (Earlier in the century, Christianity became the official religion of the Roman Empire.)

The Olympic Games were, of course, a *pagan* festival for those who worshipped more than one god. Olympia, the town where they were held, was devoted to the worship of Zeus, the most powerful of the Greek gods. The temple of Zeus at Olympia was one of the seven wonders of the ancient world. It contained a gold and ivory statue of the god that was more than 40 feet high.

The first Olympics consisted of no more than one foot race. But as time went on, the games became more and more popular, and other events were added. Held every four years, they attracted tens of thousands of people. The contestants were required to arrive at least one month in advance to train. Along with them came spectators, peddlers, gamblers, singers, dancers, and orators. They were granted safe passage through any of the city-states which happened to be at war.

A Typical Olympics. By the sixth century B.C., there were 13 Olympic events, and the contests lasted several days. The first day was devoted to worship and preparation. Both the officials and the athletes took solemn oaths. The officials swore to judge the contests fairly. The athletes swore that they would obey all the rules of competition.

On the second day the contests began.

They started with a chariot race. This was the most spectacular of all the events. It was held in an open area called the Hippodrome (HIP-uh-drome). There was only a post at each end, and the chariots had to turn around it. The distance between the posts was about 440 yards. The chariots made 12 turns around the posts for a distance of about five and a half miles.

Chariot races were very dangerous and required very skillful drivers. Each chariot was drawn by four horses abreast. Collisions on the narrow, crowded course were common. It was not unusual for only one chariot to complete the race.

When a chariot won, its owner was presented with an olive wreath, the symbol of victory at the Olympic Games. The spectators cheered and showered him with flowers. Oddly, the chariot drivers on whom everything depended received little praise.

Horse racing followed right after the chariot race. The owners of the horses were usually good riders, but, at Olympia, jockeys rode for them. Olympic horse racing wasn't fun. There were no saddles and no stirrups to hold the rider's feet. Racing bareback over a course torn up by the chariots was painful, or worse. A Greek physician in the second century A.D. wrote that "riders have often been pitched from their seats and instantly killed."

In the afternoon, the games switched to the Stadium. Like the Hippodrome, this was simply a flat area with earth embankments for the spectators to stand on. The afternoon was taken up entirely by the *pentathlon* (PEN-tath-lon). This was a contest in which each athlete had to compete in five different events. They were the discus throw, the javelin throw, the long jump, a foot race, and wrestling. The first athlete to win three events was declared the winner.

Day three of the Olympics began with religious rites. A parade of judges, priests, athletes, and trainers marched to the sacred altar of Zeus. There 100 oxen were sacrificed to the god. Their thighs were burned and the ashes added to those that had piled up over the centuries. The rest of the animals' flesh was eaten at a banquet after the games.

Some Olympic athletes competed in the five-event pentathlon. Among the events was the discus throw (right).

139

The afternoon was devoted to boys' events, which attracted athletes 12-17 years old from all over the Greek world. There were no birth certificates in those days, so the judges could not be sure of any boy's true age. They had to rely on their eyes and common sense. Besides wrestling, boys competed in the 200-meter (about 220 yards) sprint and boxing.

No Place for Women. Did women take part in the Olympic Games? They were strictly kept out, even as spectators. In ancient Greece, women were supposed to be homebodies. They did not even leave their houses to buy food. (Men did that.) There was also the question of modesty. Starting in the sixth century B.C., all contestants competed naked and barefoot. Most Greek men would not tolerate the idea of women athletes competing in the nude.

For centuries, however, Greek school girls wearing tunics competed in sports contests. By the beginning of the Christian era, races for girls were permitted at some major sports festivals. At Olympia, however, women's contests were held at a different time than the men's. Their festival honored the goddess Hera, wife of Zeus.

The last day of the Olympics began with three running events. These were the 200 meters, the 400 meters, and the long distance race of 4800 meters (about three miles). The big problem with foot races was the tendency of runners to start before the signal was given. (It is still a problem today.) Runners who "jumped the gun" at the Olympic Games could be flogged. But even this punishment did not prevent false starts. Finally a mechanical starting gate was developed to deal with the problem.

The afternoon was devoted to rough body-contact sports. These were wrestling, boxing, and the *pankration* (pan-KRAT-tee-on). The last was a combination of wrestling, judo, and boxing. All the contact sports were very popular, and all of them were brutal to some extent. In paintings and statues, Greek wrestlers are shown to be big, muscular men with thick necks.

Boxing was the roughest event of all. There were few rules of fair play. Instead of gloves, boxers had leather thongs wrapped tightly around their wrists and hands. Only the fingers were left free. There were no rounds in Olympic boxing matches, and no rest. The contestants fought continuously until one of them was knocked out or held his hands up in defeat. But winning was everything at the Olympics. Losing brought only shame. It was no wonder that the athletes prayed for "the wreath or death."

Games Go Professional. The early Olympic Games were dominated by young men of wealth. Only they could afford to hire the best coaches and spend so much time in training. But later, as athletic contests became more and more popular, there was a change. Many sports festivals vied for the best athletes. Before long, they were offering big prizes to winners. The games were no longer an

Athletes like those in this carving might have competed in the Olympic Games. Note the muscular builds of the wrestlers (center).

amusement for wealthy young men. They became an entertainment for spectators provided by professional athletes. The cash rewards made it possible for boys from the lower classes to make sports a full-time career.

Among the major sports festivals, only the Olympic Games did not offer cash prizes. However, the glory of winning at Olympia had many great rewards. Poets wrote heroic odes to the champions. Artists painted them or made statues of them. The cities from which they came held victory parades in their honor. There were financial rewards, too, provided by the cities and their rulers, and by wealthy men who enjoyed the company of athletes. When Olympic champions retired, they could count on pensions to support them comfortably for the rest of their lives.

✎ Quick Check

1. *When did the Olympic Games begin? Why did they discontinue? When? Who stopped them?*

2. *In a typical Olympics in the sixth century B.C., how many events were there? How many days did the games last?*

3. *List three events and describe their special features and differences from similar events today.*

4. *Why were women not allowed to participate or attend the games? What were the events for boys under 18?*

5. *How did the rewards of athletic competition change over the years? How did it change who could compete? What kinds of honors did Olympic winners receive?*

22
The Greeks Defeat Themselves

The people of Athens were angry. Only six miles away, Spartan soldiers were ruining Athenian farmlands. Olive trees, grape vines, and corn fields were destroyed. The young men of Athens wanted to fight the Spartans. But Pericles, the leader of Athens, told them to stay inside the city walls. He knew that the Spartan army was too strong for Athens. However, Athens' navy was second to none, and the city was rich. Pericles was sure that ships and money would defeat the Spartans. Soon the warships of Athens were raiding towns on the coast of Sparta.

Battles with Sparta. So began the war between Athens and Sparta in 431 B.C. — a war that *had* to come, people said. For many years, some Greeks had feared that Athens was getting too big, too strong, and too bossy. In 479 B.C., Athens had started a league of Greek city-states to guard against Persia. At first Athens was its leader. But soon Athens became its "boss." City-states were not allowed to quit the league. If they tried to quit, they were put down by force. They had to pay money to Athens, whether they liked it or not. The league really became Athens' empire.

Other Greek city-states were jealous of Athens' power. They feared that Athens might try to take over *all* of Greece. Sparta was especially worried by Athens. Finally, in 431 B.C., Sparta voted to go to war against Athens. Both Athens and Sparta had many allies among the city-states. The allies came into the war too. The war lasted almost 30 years and was very hard. Little mercy was shown by either side. Many innocent people were killed as Greeks fought Greeks.

Athens' suffering was very great. The farmers who grew food for Athens had to move inside the city walls when the war began. The city became very crowded. Most of the farmers had to sleep in the streets, in temples, or in huts.

Pericles Rallys Citizens. The people of Athens blamed Pericles for all their troubles. They wanted to make peace with Sparta. They said that Pericles had dragged them into the war. They shook their fists at him and cursed him.

Pericles gave them his answer in a speech. He reminded them of their duty to defend Athens. If the city fell, he said, they would all be ruined. Then he reminded them that they too had voted for the war. He accused them of being weak and not able to take setbacks. Finally, he reminded them that they had a great empire. "Half the world is yours—the sea," he said. The people of Athens must defend that empire or become slaves. Pericles told them to be worthy of their past glory.

The Athenians were won over by Pericles' speech. They agreed to go on with the war against Sparta. But a year later, in 429 B.C., Pericles died. He died of an awful sickness that spread over the city. About one person in every four died. Dead bodies were piled up in the streets.

The war went on for many years. Sometimes Athens seemed to be winning. At other times Sparta seemed to be winning. Finally, in 404 B.C., Athens had to surrender. The walls of the city were torn down. Athens now had to obey cruel rulers chosen by the Spartans. The Golden Age of Athens was over.

✎ **Quick Check**

1. *Why did the city-states become dissatisfied with Athens' leadership of the league? Which city-state headed the opposition?*

2. *Who was the leader of Athens? How did he convince the citizens to unite behind him?*

3. *How long did the city-states fight each other? What was the outcome?*

23
Alexander the Great

The long, bloody war between Athens and Sparta left the city-states of Greece without strength. Even Sparta was too weak to control Greece for long. Other city-states rose against Sparta. In 371 B.C., Sparta was defeated by Thebes (theebz). It was never again a great power.

The real winner of the wars among the Greeks was an outsider. King Philip the Second of Macedonia (mas-uh-DOE-nee-uh), a land to the north, defeated the weakened cities of Greece. By 338 B.C., Philip was the supreme ruler of Greece.

Two years later, Philip gave a great feast for his daughter's wedding. Many Greeks had come to honor him. There was music, dancing, games, and lots of food. Just as Philip was about to watch some plays, an assassin pulled out a dagger. He stabbed Philip to death before guards could stop him.

The people in the theater started to panic. Then a handsome young man of 20 spoke to them from the stage. He told them to stay calm. "Nothing has changed," he said, "except the name of the king." The people cheered. Soldiers crowded around him, for this young man was Philip's son, Alexander, the next king of Macedonia. In a few years, he would defeat and rule Persia, the largest empire in the world. He would be called Alexander the Great.

What was this young king like? He had already shown that he was a good soldier. At 18 he had helped his father defeat Greek armies and had fought bravely. Yet no man admired the Greeks more than Alexander. The Greeks had

given the world its greatest poets, writers, and thinkers. Alexander read all their books. He even slept with a book of Greek poetry under his pillow. His teacher was the best thinker in all Greece, Aristotle. From him, Alexander learned Greek ideas of right and wrong, and politics.

Conquering Persia. Alexander knew what he wanted to do. Once the great empire of Persia had tried to defeat the Greeks. Now Alexander would lead the Macedonians and Greeks against Persia. He was sure he would win. Then he would set up new Greek cities all over the Persian Empire. He would make almost the whole world Greek, and he, Alexander, would rule it!

In the spring of 334 B.C., Alexander led his army of 40,000 men into Asia. He was only 22 years old. His army carried heavy weapons of war. There were

- towers on wheels to attack high walls;
- battering rams to break down walls;
- large catapults, or slings, to throw heavy rocks;
- small catapults that threw several spears at once.

The Persians were once again led by a king named Darius. But the King Darius of Alexander's time was not as great a warrior as the earlier King Darius. Alexander's army met Darius's army in Asia Minor. Alexander's mounted soldiers broke the Persian lines, and Darius ran away. Darius's mother, wife, and two daughters were taken prisoner.

Soon after, Darius wrote to Alexander. He asked Alexander to return his family to him. He offered Alexander friendship in return. Alexander's answer was very tough. He said Darius would have to ask him in person for his family. And Darius would have to treat him as "lord of all Asia." If not, Alexander wrote, "stand your ground and fight for it. Do not run away, for I will chase you any place you go."

Alexander did chase the Persian king and finally found him—dead. He had been murdered by one of his own men. Alexander had Darius buried in a royal tomb, and he showed no mercy to Darius's murderer.

Ruling Diverse Lands. Alexander had won the largest empire in the world, but could he hold it by force alone? Alexander knew it would be impossible. He had to win the friendship of the Persians to keep peace in his empire. Soon Alexander began to treat Persians as the equals of Greeks and Macedonians. He took many Persians into his army and his government. Alexander married a daughter of Darius and often wore Persian clothes. He had 10,000 of his soldiers marry Persian women!

In just 11 years, a fearless young Macedonian, later called Alexander the Great, won a vast empire.

Many of Alexander's officers became angry with him. They thought he was being too friendly to the Persians. They refused to fight for him anymore and asked to go home. One of them told him:

"This, Alexander, is what hurts us: You have made Persians your kinsmen (relatives), and they are allowed to kiss you. But no Macedonian has this right."

Alexander answered quickly. "But all of you are my kinsmen," he said, "and from now on I will call you so."

Later Alexander gave a feast. Thousands of Macedonians, Greeks, and Persians drank wine from the same bowls.

Alexander's Legacy. It had taken Alexander 11 years to win his great empire. It stretched from Greece in the west into India in the east. He had fought hard and had many wounds. He had often gone without food or water. In June 323 B.C., he was in the city of Babylon. He was planning to explore the coast of Arabia, but he suddenly became sick. In a few days, Alexander the Great was dead. The man who had ruled "the world" was not yet 33 years old.

Alexander the Great left behind him about 70 new Greek cities in the old Persian Empire. In these cities, Greek learning was preserved.

One of these cities, Alexandria in Egypt, became the leading center of trade and learning in the ancient world. But later Alexandria came under the rule of a great new empire led by Rome. The city of Rome passed Alexandria in wealth and power. Rome became the greatest city in the world.

✎ Quick Check

1. *What outside nation became the real winner of the wars between the city-states of Greece? Who was its leader?*

2. *Who was Alexander? What was his attitude toward the Greeks? Who was his teacher?*

3. *What was Alexander's first big military campaign? What kind of equipment did he bring? Who was the enemy's leader, and what did he do in the heat of battle?*

4. *How did Alexander unite his empire? What problems did it cause? How large was his empire when he died? What was its main city?*

MAP EXERCISE

At his death in 323 B.C., Alexander's empire stretched east from Macedonia and Greece into India. Use this map to answer the following questions:

1. How great a distance was it from Athens to the delta of the Indus River?

2. Name three lands in Alexander's empire that had once been ruled by other great civilizations.

THE EMPIRE OF ALEXANDER THE GREAT

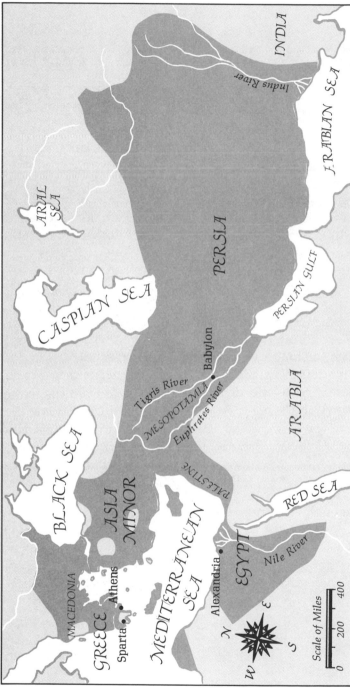

ARAL SEA

CASPIAN SEA

PERSIA

INDIA

Indus River

ARABIAN SEA

PERSIAN GULF

Babylon

Tigris River

MESOPOTAMIA

Euphrates River

ARABIA

BLACK SEA

ASIA MINOR

PALESTINE

RED SEA

MACEDONIA

GREECE

Athens

Sparta

MEDITERRANEAN SEA

Alexandria

EGYPT

Nile River

N

E

S

W

Scale of Miles

0   200   400

PART 4
Review and Skills Exercises

| 3000 | A | 2000 | B | C | 1000 | DE | FGHI | B.C. |

Putting Events in Order

Part 4 described ancient Greece and the formation of the first democratic government. The differences between the two great city-states of Sparta and Athens led to a long war that weakened all of Greece. On the time line above, letters are placed on the approximate dates when certain important events took place. Below is a list of events that took place during the time period shown on the time line. The events are not in order. Decide which event belongs with each letter, A-I. Write the letters on a sheet of paper. By each letter write the description of the proper event.

- Greek city-states develop; dark age of Greece ends.
- Greek civilization starts; early communities are ruled by kings.
- War begins between Sparta and Athens; lasts 27 years.
- Alexander marches against Persia.
- Philip of Macedonia conquers Greece.
- Minoan civilization begins.
- Dorians conquer early Greeks; dark age of Greece begins.
- List of Olympic winners first kept.
- Greeks defeat Persians at Marathon; Golden Age of Greece begins.

150

Making Inferences

Have you heard the phrase "reading between the lines"? Reading between the lines is a way of making an interpretation based on ideas or facts you have read. You infer or interpret something that is not stated directly. Consider this paragraph from Part 4:

> Greek colonies in Asia Minor rebelled against Persian rule. They asked Athens to help. Athens sent 20 warships to Asia Minor. These ships helped the rebels to burn a Persian city.

Although it is not stated directly, we can infer from the paragraph that Athens sympathized with the Greek colonies who wanted to overthrow the Persians. The fact that Athens sent 20 warships tells us that Athens was willing to help.

The passage that follows is from *A History of the Peloponnesian War*, a detailed account of the long struggle between Athens and Sparta that began around 430 B.C. The author of the work was Thucydides, an Athenian soldier and historian. Read the passage and follow the directions below.

> In the same winter the Athenians, following their annual custom, gave a public funeral for those who had been the first to die in the war. These funerals are held in

the following way: Two days before the ceremony the bones of the fallen are brought and put in a tent which has been erected, and people make whatever offerings they wish to their own dead. Then there is a funeral procession in which coffins of cypress wood are carried on wagons. There is one coffin for each tribe, which contains the bones of members of that tribe. One empty bier is decorated and carried in the procession; this is for the missing whose bodies could not be recovered. Everyone who wishes to, both citizens and foreigners, can join in the procession, and the women who are related to the dead are there to make their laments at the tomb. The bones are laid in the public burial-place, which is in the most beautiful quarter outside the city walls. Here the Athenians always bury those who have fallen in war. The only exception is those who died at Marathon, who, because their achievement was considered absolutely outstanding, were buried on the battlefield itself.

Below each statement are possible inferences to complete the statement. Write number 1-4 on a sheet of paper. By each number write the letter of the inference you think is correct for each statement.

1. Athens' official policy was to

   a. *bury everyone with a public ceremony.*
   b. *honor those first to die in war.*
   c. *make cemeteries very beautiful.*

2. In Athens people were considered

   a. *members of different groups or tribes.*
   b. *members of Greek fraternities.*
   c. *heroes of Marathon.*

3. An honored soldier was buried

   a. *in a coffin.*

   b. *on the battlefield.*
   c. *within the city walls.*

4. The funeral for the war dead

   a. *lasted several days and was a very important event.*
   b. *was attended by men only.*
   c. *was for the families of the fallen only.*

Building Vocabulary Using Context Clues

The words below are taken from the passage by Thucydides. See if you can guess the meaning of each word by its context, or the way the word is used in relation to the words around it. Study the three possible definitions for each word. Write the numbers 1-5 on a sheet of paper. By each number write the word and then the definition that best fits the word. When you have finished, check your choices in a dictionary.

1. custom

   common practice   duty   festival

2. offerings

   something given as a tribute or for worship
   something offered for sale
   a bid on something for sale

3. bier

   statue   coffin   urn

4. laments

   cries of grief
   prayers of thanksgiving
   silent processions

5. quarter

   a division or part of a city or town
   half of something
   a unit of money

151

THE ROMAN
REPUBLIC

They were brave, they were tough, and they were patriotic. They believed above all in duty and loyalty to Rome. In times of peace they farmed the land. In times of war they defended it against all enemies. These people, the early Romans, had many heroes who were models of courage and virtue. One of them was a commander named Marcus Atilius Regulus. In 255 B.C., Regulus led an attack against Rome's enemy, Carthage, in North Africa. His forces were defeated, however, and Regulus was taken prisoner.

After five years, Carthage sent him back to Rome on a peace mission. Regulus promised his captors that if his mission failed, he would return to Carthage as a prisoner. In Rome, Regulus urged the Senate (legislature) not to make peace with Carthage, but to fight on. Then, true to his promise, he returned to Carthage. There he was tortured and put to death.

Heroes like Regulus helped Rome to become the greatest power the ancient world had ever known. In time, its empire became even larger than that of Alexander the Great. It took in all the land around the Mediterranean Sea and more. For hundreds of years, the center of this empire was Italy and the city of Rome. The empire included hundreds of nationalities and tribes with almost 100 million people.

The early city of Rome was ruled by the Etruscans, a people with an advanced civilization in the northern half of Italy. In 509 B.C., the Romans revolted against their Etruscan masters and drove them out. Rome became an independent republic controlled by a nobility of wealthy landowners.

Members of the nobility were known as *patricians* (pah-TRISH-unz). Leading patricians made up the Senate. Every year the Senate elected two *consuls* from the patrician class to serve as executives of the state.

The great majority of Romans were not patricians. They were known as *plebeians* (plih-BEE-yenz), or common people. The plebeians had their own popular assembly, but it could only advise the Senate. Real power was wielded by the patricians.

The concentration of power in the patrician class reflected Roman society. It was centered on the family, in which the authority of the father was absolute. Roman children learned the importance of obedience and respect from an early age. They were also taught to admire legendary heroes and try to be like them. One of these heroes was Cincinnatus, a farmer who was born about 519 B.C. Twice Cincinnatus left his plow to lead Roman soldiers in victorious battles. Both times he refused all honors and political power. Instead he returned to his farm.

Farmer-soldiers like Cincinnatus were the backbone of the armies that defeated Rome's enemies. Gradually Roman rule was extended over all of Italy. Rome's liberal treatment of defeated Italian tribes won it many loyal allies.

Roman expansion soon brought it into conflict with Carthage, a powerful city-state in North Africa. It was founded by Phoenicians about 800 B.C. near the present city of Tunis. From 264 to 146 B.C. Rome fought three long wars with Carthage for control of the western Mediterranean. (They were called the Punic Wars. "Punic" was a form of the Greek word for Phoenician.)

These wars ended in the complete defeat and destruction of Carthage. At the same time, Rome also brought Macedonia and the Greek city-states under its rule. Rome was now the master of most of the Mediterranean world.

The growth of the empire created tensions within the government. There were more and bigger decisions to make. Feuds broke out between the plebeians and patricians. This period of unrest lasted almost 100 years. Then a powerful leader appeared: Julius Caesar (JEWL-yus SEE-zur). He reduced the power of the Senate. After Caesar, consuls would no longer rule, only emperors.

24

The Etruscans, Teachers of Rome

Many Greeks were horrified. A Greek scholar named Theopompus (thee-oh-POMP-uss) had visited northern Italy. He studied the culture of the Etruscans (ih-TRUSS-kunz) who lived there. When he returned to Greece, he told tales of an immoral people. They thought of nothing but luxury. To the Greeks, who believed in living simply, the Etruscans sounded disgusting.

Theopompus was most critical of Etruscan women. He said that they deceived their husbands, and they tried to act like men. Certainly, Etruscan women must have seemed strange to him after living in Greece. Athenian women led very limited lives. They had to stay at home all the time. They could not go to school. They were not allowed to talk to men who were not relatives. Only men could own property in Greece.

Etruscan women were much freer. They could go out alone. They ate with men and learned to read. Sometimes they owned property. A few Etruscan male leaders were greatly influenced by their wives.

Historians know now that Theopompus made up many of his stories. Why? At this time, around 340 B.C., the Greeks were hostile toward the Etruscans. The Greek navy had tried to take control of the western Mediterranean Sea. It failed because the Etruscan navy was too powerful. The Etruscans chased the Greek ships back to Greece and treated all cap-

A wall painting from a fifth century B.C. Etruscan tomb shows musicians wearing typical clothing. Page 152: Later citizens of the Roman Empire owed many cultural debts to the sophisticated Etruscans.

tured Greeks mercilessly. Perhaps Theopompus's imagination was influenced by his prejudices.

Comfortable Living. Despite their differences, the Etruscans admired and imitated the Greeks. They grew grapes and olives, sculpted, made beautiful jewelry, and used the Greek alphabet. However, many Etruscans, including some slaves, lived in the kind of comfort that the Greeks avoided. They had large houses made of clay and wood. The houses even had plumbing. Sometimes they were covered in brightly painted tiles.

Rich Etruscans were very sociable. They ate two lavish meals a day with friends and neighbors. Both men and women dressed up for meals. The men wore thin woolen cloaks and shoes with laces. The women wore colorful linen tunics, heavy gold jewelry, and makeup. Slaves served rich food and wine diluted with water. After dinner there was music and dancing.

Where did the Etruscans come from, and how did they become so wealthy? Most historians believe that they came from Asia Minor by sea in the seventh century B.C. They settled in northern Italy, in an area called Etruria (eh-TROO-ree-uh). There they established 12 small city-states. At roughly the same time, a tribe called the Latins came from an area north of Italy and established a small settlement south of Etruria which they called Rome.

Etruscans grew prosperous from trading with other nations and from growing crops of grains, fruits, and vegetables. Farming was very easy because there was plenty of sun, rain, and fertile soil. A person could also get rich from mining and, sometimes, by becoming a pirate. Etruscan pirates were feared throughout the Mediterranean.

Rule Over Rome. The Romans and the Etruscans lived side by side in an uneasy peace for almost three centuries. The Etruscans taught the Romans some of the things that they had learned from the Greeks. They also showed the Romans how to build aqueducts, houses, bridges, and temples.

In 616 B.C., the first Etruscan king ascended the throne of Rome. A line of Etruscan kings ruled over Rome for over a century. The last Etruscan king, Tarquin the Proud, was harsh and corrupt. Roman citizens revolted against him in 509

B.C. The Etruscan rule of Rome was ended. During the next two centuries, the Romans gained control of the Etruscan city-states. In 87 B.C., all Etruscans became Roman citizens.

Why did the Etruscans lose their power to Rome? To begin with, their city-states were never really united. They often fought each other. When Tarquin the Proud was trying to regain his throne, some of the city-states refused to help him, because they were angry with his native city-state. In addition, Roman citizens were unhappy about having a king. A group of rich patricians wanted to form their own government. They established the Roman Republic.

✎ **Quick Check**

1. *Who was Theopompus? What did he say about the Etruscans? Give two reasons why he did not tell the truth.*

2. *Where was Etruria? Where did its people come from? When? What were two differences between the Etruscans and the Greeks?*

3. *What people settled to the south of Etruria? What was their settlement called?*

4. *During what period did the Etruscans rule Rome? How did Roman rule come about? What happened to the Etruscans?*

MAP EXERCISE

The Etruscan people greatly influenced Romans partly because their land was so close to Rome. Use this map to answer the following questions:

1. How far would a trade ship have to travel to reach Carthage from Rome?

2. What Etrurian city was on the Adriatic

Sea? What was the southernmost Etrurian city?

ITALY, SIXTH CENTURY B.C.

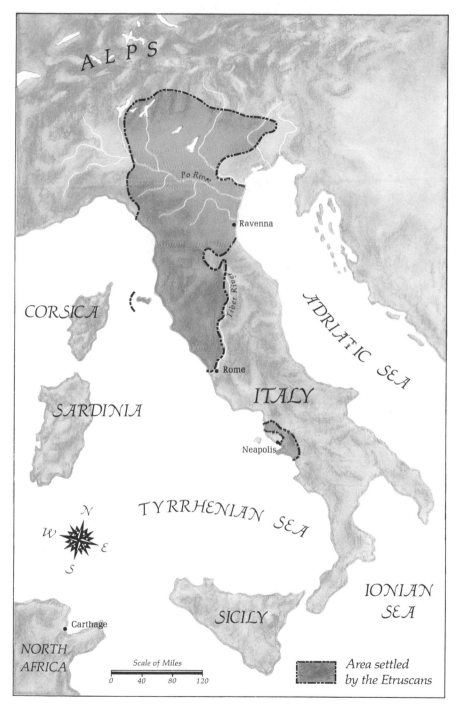

ALPS

Po River

Ravenna

Tiber River

CORSICA

ADRIATIC SEA

SARDINIA

Rome

ITALY

Neapolis

TYRRHENIAN SEA

N
W · E
S

IONIAN
SEA

SICILY

Carthage

NORTH
AFRICA

Scale of Miles

0   40   80   120

Area settled
by the Etruscans

25
A Father's Choice

Rome began as a group of villages on the Tiber (TIE-bur) River. Some time in the eighth century B.C., these villages became a town—Rome. As we have seen, it was first ruled by Etruscan kings. But the Latins rebelled and freed themselves. This chapter tells of an incident in this war of freedom. Which value did Brutus place higher: loyalty to his city-state or protection of his children? Was his decision the right one?

The young men were tied to wooden poles. Their clothes were ripped off, and they were beaten with sticks. But the worst was still to come. For these young men were traitors to Rome. Their final punishment would be death.

All of these young men came from rich and noble families. Two of them were sons of Junius Brutus (JUNE-ee-us BROO-tus), the Roman consul (elected government leader). Brutus had the power to pardon these traitors. Would he do it? Or would he let his own sons die as an example to others? The Roman crowd watched Brutus closely. They knew how much he was suffering, and they pitied him.

What was Brutus thinking at this moment? Did he think of Tarquin (TAR-kwin) the Proud, the former king of Rome? Brutus hated all that Tarquin stood for. Tarquin was an Etruscan. Although most of the Etruscan leaders of Rome had been fair, Tarquin was not.

Brutus hated Tarquin for his cruel, one-man rule. Tarquin did not ask the Roman

Senate for its advice. Tarquin made war or peace without asking these Roman leaders for their opinions. He had put some Roman senators to death and had taken the property of others. As a crowning insult, Tarquin's son had raped Lucretia (loo-KREE-shuh), a virtuous Roman wife.

Finally, in 509 B.C., Brutus swore that he would get rid of Tarquin. He stirred up a revolt. The angry people drove Tarquin and his sons out of Rome. Then the people elected Brutus and another man consuls. Rome became a republic. It would have no more kings.

But Tarquin did not give up easily. He knew that many young nobles did not like the republic. Under the king, they had received special treatment. If they broke a law, the king often forgave them. But in the republic, the law treated rich and poor as equals.

Sons Caught in Plot. So Tarquin sent agents to some of these young nobles in Rome. And they promised to help Tarquin become king again. Two of them were the sons of Brutus. But the young nobles made a bad mistake. They wrote letters to Tarquin saying they would hand over Rome to him. A slave found

This wall sculpture charts a Roman boy's progress from infancy to boyhood. In the scene at right he recites lessons to his father.

161

The early Romans, farmers who worked hard and lived simply, built their empire bit by bit. They were skilled builders and some of their early structures still stand.

these letters and showed them to Brutus. Brutus arrested all the young nobles and put them in prison. Later they were sentenced to die as traitors.

Brutus was in charge of carrying out the sentence. When the day came, everyone watched him. Would he let his own sons die?

Probably Brutus wished to forgive them. But his duty was to punish traitors. He hid his suffering. He did not blink while the traitors were beheaded.

Was Brutus a hard man? Perhaps. But the early Romans had to be tough. The small city-state was fighting for its life against enemies who were all around the area. The early Romans were farmers who worked hard and lived simply. But when Rome was attacked, they quickly left their farms and became soldiers. They had courage and a strong sense of duty.

Lessons of Family Life. Romans learned the importance of duty and loyalty as children at home. In the Roman family, the father had complete power. His wife and children had to obey him in everything. He arranged the marriages of his sons and daughters and controlled their property. He had the right to kill a child who did not obey him. He also had the right to sell a child into slavery. Roman fathers did not use these powers often. But it was enough that they had them. Roman children learned early to obey and respect their fathers. Later their fathers taught them to have the same obedience and respect for Rome.

✎ **Quick Check**

1. Who was Tarquin? What kind of a leader was he?

2. Who was Brutus? What type of government did he help establish in Rome? When?

3. Why did Brutus's sons and other young nobles try to return Tarquin to the throne? What was the result of their efforts?

4. What was the livelihood of the early Romans? How was family life governed? How was it similar to people's attitudes toward the government?

26
Hannibal Against Rome

A great army was marching against Rome. It had about 50,000 foot soldiers and 9,000 soldiers on horseback. As it marched, the army was seven miles long. Behind the soldiers were 37 big war elephants. And behind them were the many animals that carried supplies.

The leader of this army was a young general named Hannibal Barca (HAN-uh-bull BAR-cuh). Hannibal came from Carthage, a rich and powerful city-state in North Africa. Rome and Carthage had fought a long war for control of the island of Sicily (SIS-uh-lee). Finally, Carthage was forced to give up Sicily and two other islands to Rome.

Hannibal was only a boy when this happened. But his father, Hamilcar (HAM-ill-kar) Barca, the top general of Carthage, made him take an oath. Hannibal swore that some day he would get revenge against the enemy, Rome.

The Great March. Carthage began to rebuild its armies in Spain, one of its colonies. It hired professional soldiers from North Africa, Spain, and islands in the Mediterranean. Hannibal became the commander of these soldiers when he was 26 years old. His men were all for him. They knew he was a great soldier and afraid of nothing. He wore a simple officer's uniform and often slept on the ground near them. Hannibal could count on their loyalty to the end.

Hannibal had a daring and secret plan of war against Rome. He wanted to fight the Romans on their own ground. The Roman navy was too strong for him to risk moving his army to Italy in ships.

But there was another way for him to reach Italy. He could march his army 1,500 miles overland to get there. This meant that his army would have to cross the Alps, the highest mountains in Eu-

rope. It would be dangerous, but Hannibal was not afraid of danger.

The long march began in May 218 B.C. From Spain, Hannibal's army moved across the south of France. One of Hannibal's first problems was to get his elephants across a wide river. Big rafts were built to ferry them across. But some of the elephants panicked on the rafts. They began to stamp and scream with fear. Some fell into the river, but they did not drown. They walked across, with only their trunks sticking up above the water.

Finally Hannibal's army reached the Alps. The mountains were covered with snow and ice. The cold and wind chilled the men to their bones. Many became sick and were left behind.

The path through the Alps was narrow, twisting, and very steep. Men and animals slipped and fell thousands of feet to their deaths. Often they could not see ahead of them because of snow storms. Blinded by snow, tired, and dizzy from hunger, the men stumbled on.

Then one day the men looked down and saw a green valley below them. They had made it across the Alps to Italy. The long march had taken five months. Probably half of those who had started out had died. Those who made it were worn out. But after a long rest, they got back their strength.

The Romans were amazed when they learned that Hannibal was in Italy. They sent one army after another to capture him. Usually the Roman armies were much larger than Hannibal's. But Hannibal was such a clever general that he defeated them all. In one battle, he led the Roman army into a trap. The Romans were then surrounded and wiped out.

Hannibal could defeat Roman armies, but he could not attack the city of Rome itself. His army was not strong enough for that. So the war dragged on for 15 years. Meanwhile, Hannibal's army burned and destroyed much of the land.

Hannibal's Defeat. Finally, the Romans found a way to get rid of Hannibal. They sent an army to North Africa to attack Carthage. This army was led by a young general, Scipio (SIP-ee-oh), who knew all of Hannibal's tricks. Carthage then called Hannibal home to defend it against Scipio. This is what Rome wanted. In 202 B.C. Scipio defeated Hannibal. Carthage had to make peace with Rome and give up Spain.

What happened to Hannibal? He ran away to the Middle East where he tried to stir up trouble for Rome. Years later, Roman agents closed in on him. Hannibal, now 65, swallowed poison and died.

What happened to Carthage? The Romans always feared that Carthage might become dangerous again. A Roman senator named Cato (KATE-oh) said over and over, "Carthage must be destroyed." Finally, in 146 B.C., a Roman army completely destroyed the city of Carthage. North Africa became a part of Rome's growing empire.

✎ **Quick Check**

1. *Where was Carthage? Over what island did it fight with Rome? Who won?*

2. *Who was Hannibal? What did he take an oath to do?*

3. *What was Hannibal's bold plan? Why did he choose such a difficult plan? How large was his army?*

4. *How long did Hannibal remain in Italy? Did his mission succeed? How did he die?*

5. *Who was Cato? What was his concern? What did Rome do about it?*

HANNIBAL'S ROUTE

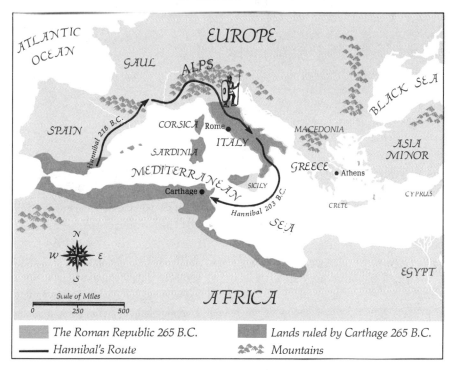

The Roman Republic 265 B.C.
Hannibal's Route
Lands ruled by Carthage 265 B.C.
Mountains

MAP EXERCISE

Hannibal avoided doing battle with the superior Roman navy by marching his army over land. Use the map to answer the following questions:

1. In 265 B.C., Carthage controlled part of the northern coast of which continent? The southern coast of which modern-day country? Which islands?

2. From which country did Hannibal and his army begin their long march to Rome? In what directions did they travel?

3. How many years went by between the time Hannibal started out for Rome and the time he left Italy to return to Carthage?

27
Conqueror Learns from Conquered

Rome was now a great power. It had taken over all of Italy. It had defeated Carthage. It had taken control of Greece.

The Greeks were the conquered. The Romans were the conquerors. But the conquered had something to teach the conquerors. The following conversation explains what it was.

The year: 140 B.C.

The place: a street in Rome.

The action: a rich Roman, Flavius (FLAY-vee-us), and his new Greek slave, Theodorus (thee-oh-DOR-us), are taking a walk.

FLAVIUS: Theodorus, let me tell you why I want you to serve my family.

THEODORUS: Please do, sir.

FLAVIUS: The truth is, there is much I admire in you. I wish that I had gone to school like you. My father taught me all I know at home. And what was that? A little reading, writing, and arithmetic. Mainly he taught me the old Roman ways: duty to my family, loyalty to Rome, and respect for the gods. Such things are very good in their own way, Theodorus, I will not deny that. But I'll be very honest. Compared to you Greeks, we Romans are really a little rough and crude.

THEODORUS: In certain ways I agree with you, sir. If you will pardon me for saying so, some Romans still behave a little like barbarians. The things that

The conquered Greeks taught their Roman conquerers to love stage drama. This Greek wall painting shows actors celebrating their success.

168

Romans do sometimes shock me. In my hometown in Greece, I saw Roman soldiers tear down a beautiful painting. And do you know what they did with it? They put it on the ground and played dice on it!

FLAVIUS: That's just what I mean, Theodorus. Now you Greeks are so different. Look at all you know about art and history and poetry. Look at all you know about science and politics. How much you admire wisdom, and how interested you are in ideas! We Romans are very good at war. We are good at building roads and bridges and stadiums. But have we ever had a man as wise as Socrates? Have we ever had a poet like Homer? Or a man who writes plays like Euripides?

THEODORUS: That is quite true, sir. But you haven't told me yet why you wanted me to serve your family.

FLAVIUS: I'm coming to that, Theodorus, I'm coming to that. You see, I want my children to have a real education. I want them to have all the things I never had. They must study music, poetry, plays, good books, and science. I want them to have knowledge, Theodorus. My sons must learn the art of making speeches, in case they want to go into politics. These are all things that you can teach them, Theodorus. That's why I bought you in the first place. Do you understand?

THEODORUS: I understand you very well, sir. But what about the old Roman ways of duty and loyalty? What about working hard and living simply? Do you want me to teach those to your children?

FLAVIUS: Oh, of course, Theodorus. But let's be honest. Times are changing. My father was a simple farmer. To him, all those things were very important. "Be a good soldier and obey your leaders," he always said. "The rest will take care of itself." And I did as I was told. But you can't expect children to believe all that stuff now, Theodorus. They've been spoiled.

When I was a boy, I lived in a house that had only one room. We ate and slept in that one room. But later I made a lot of money in farming. Then I bought a fine house in Rome.

So how can I tell my children to live simply? How can I tell them to work hard when they already have everything they want? What do they care about ideas such as duty and loyalty to the state? They like to be free and to enjoy the good things in life. I'm afraid they will become very soft. But at least they will have learning.

✎ Quick Check

1. *Who are Flavius and Theodorus? What does Flavius want Theodorus to do?*

2. *What kind of upbringing did Flavius have? How was it different from his children's? What does he fear for them, and what is his remedy?*

3. *What differences between the Greeks and the Romans are presented in the chapter?*

28
Caesar: Three Views

Rome was a republic; it had no kings. But it was not very democratic. Most of the power was in the hands of the Senate. Its members were patricians, and most of them were rich landowners.

For many years, the plebeians fought for a greater voice in the government. They won many important rights and elected their own leaders. But wealthy Romans kept control of the Senate.

All of Rome's wars hurt its farmers badly. They were soldiers and had to leave the farms to fight. Many were ruined by the wars.

Soon, plebeian leaders began to fight with patrician leaders for control of the government. A bloody civil war broke out. It lasted, on and off, for more than a century.

Finally, a Roman general named Julius Caesar (JEWL-yus SEE-zur) took power. The Senate became helpless.

Caesar was no ordinary man. To his soldiers, he was almost a god. To plebeians, he was a great hero. To the Senate, he was an evil man who wished to be king.

Suppose that you are in the Roman Forum (the main public meeting place) in 45 B.C. Here is what some of the people are saying about Caesar:

ROMAN SOLDIER: I served with Caesar for eight years in Gaul (modern France). I tell you there is not a greater general

*After a century of civil war in Rome, Julius Caesar took control of the republic.
Several years later in 44 B.C., a group of angry senators murdered him.*

172

or a braver man anywhere. Many times the enemy had three soldiers or more for every Roman soldier. Often we were sure the enemy would defeat us.

Once we had to fight an army of very tough Germans. These Germans were hired by the Gauls to fight for them. Before the battle, we were so scared that we made out our wills. The officers begged Caesar to turn back. But Caesar reminded them of the times that Roman soldiers had smashed German armies. He said he was ready to fight with only one legion (6,000 men), if necessary. He made us feel so ashamed, we could not wait for the battle to start.

During the battle, Caesar was everywhere, urging us on. Once he saw some men who were about to give up. He grabbed a shield and ordered them to follow him. At once, the men began to fight again behind Caesar. Finally the Germans broke and ran for their lives!

Yes, Caesar shared all our dangers. He fought with us, ate with us, and lived with us. I would fight for him again anytime, any place.

ROMAN WORKER: Julius Caesar has done more for plebeians than any other Roman. Sure he is a noble and very rich. But he has always been for the poor. Look at all the things he has done for us. When he became dictator, he gave us a holiday that lasted for 10 days. He spent a fortune to entertain us. There were big parades and sports events the whole time. In one stadium alone, 400 lions were killed by the gladiators. In another, the soldiers put on a big make-believe battle. And there were plays in all the theaters.

One day Caesar gave a party for 20,000 poor people. He gave them money, bread, and oil for their lamps. He was even more generous to his soldiers. He gave each of them some land to farm.

Since then, Caesar has given jobs to army veterans and helped people who owe money. He has even allowed some very poor people to stop paying their rent. Now he is planning to build new roads, canals, temples, and theaters. Think of all the jobs that will give to the Romans who are out of work! Yes, Julius Caesar is a great man. He is the best friend the common people ever had.

ROMAN SENATOR: Julius Caesar is the most dangerous man that Rome has ever seen. He doesn't really care about the poor people. He just buys their support by giving them shows and handing out bread. The only thing Caesar cares about is power, power for himself. Sure, it was the Senate which voted to make him dictator. But what could we do? Caesar had the army and the common people behind him. We were helpless. We had to make him dictator, or else. No one could stop

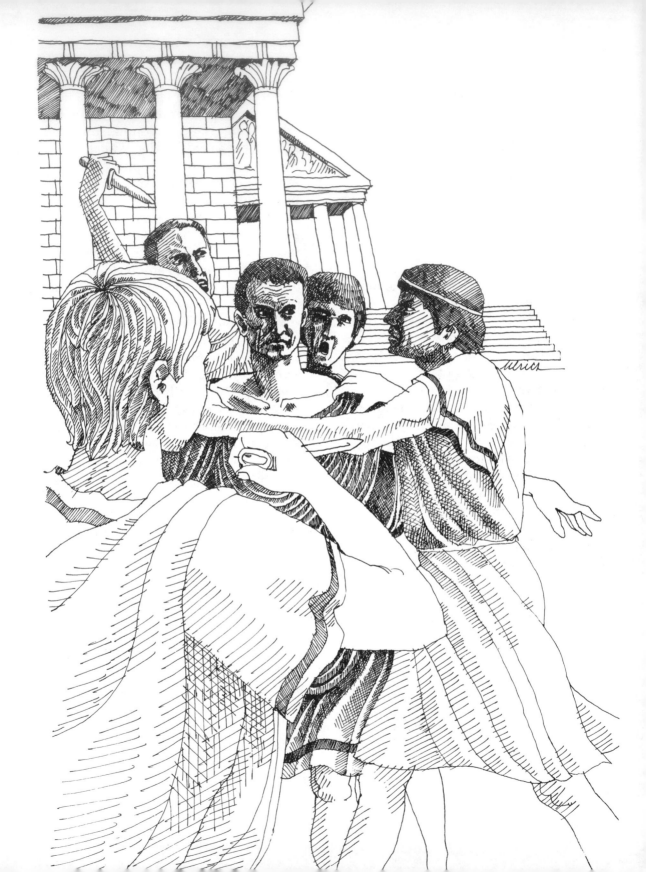

him from taking power. Now he treats even the greatest senators as if they were beggars. Soon he will want to be king! Then he will get rid of the Senate, and there will be no more voting by the people. Yes, the republic is in danger as long as Caesar lives. We must save the republic and get rid of this evil man.

Caesar's Murder. Many other senators thought the same way about Caesar. In 44 B.C., 50 of them joined in a plot to kill Caesar. One was a man Caesar had always liked, Marcus Brutus (MAR-cus BRUTE-us).

The day picked for the murder was March 15. That day, Caesar paid a visit to the Senate. One senator asked Caesar for a special favor. Caesar said no. Then the senator pulled back Caesar's robe, showing his neck and chest. That was the signal for murder.

Other senators rushed at Caesar with daggers and began to stab him. At first, Caesar tried to defend himself. But then he saw Brutus come at him. "You too, my friend?" he asked Brutus. Then he covered his face with his robe as Brutus stabbed him to death.

The murder of Caesar did not save the republic. By 30 B.C., Caesar's adopted son, Octavian, took complete power in Rome. Octavian became Rome's first emperor. The Roman Republic was gone. The Roman Empire took its place.

✎ Quick Check

1. *What two groups were struggling for power when Julius Caesar took over? Which group(s) liked him? Why? Which group(s) did not? Why?*

2. *What kind of government did Rome have under Caesar? What was Caesar called? Why?*

3. *Who murdered Caesar? Why? When? Who succeeded him? What happened to the republic?*

PART 5
Review and Skills Exercises

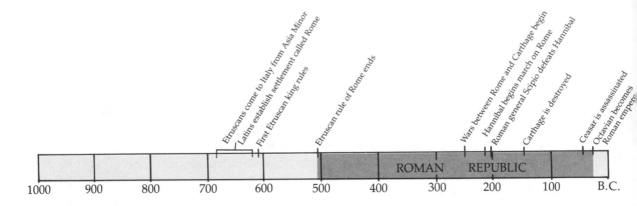

Understanding Events

In Part 5, you have read how Etruscan rule gave way to Roman rule and the establishment of the republic. The Senate took over some of the king's power then gave it up as Rome grew unwieldy. Study the time line above, and then answer the questions that follow. On a sheet of paper write the numbers 1-5. By each number write *true* if the statement is true and *false* if the statement is not true.

1. The Roman Republic was established in the sixth century B.C.

2. The destruction of Carthage took place more than two centuries before Caesar was assassinated.

3. The Etruscans appeared on the Italian peninsula in the fourth century B.C.

4. Etruscan rule of Rome ended in 509 B.C.

5. The time line contains events that occurred in the first century A.D.

Using Writing Skills

Writing a good paragraph is a skill that is important whether you are answering an essay question, writing a report, or writing a letter to a friend. A good paragraph is one that states information in a clear way. A good paragraph may contain a topic sentence that states the main idea of the paragraph. The topic sentence is backed up by supporting details that explain the main idea. Follow the directions below to practice finding and writing good paragraphs. Write your answers to the questions on a sheet of paper.

1. In Chapter 24 on the Etruscans, find the paragraph on page 157 that begins

176

with this sentence, "Rich Etruscans were very sociable."

a. Explain why this sentence is a topic sentence for the paragraph.

b. List any supporting details in the paragraph that explain the topic sentence.

2. Locate another paragraph in Part 5 that contains a topic sentence and supporting details. Write the page number and topic sentence on your paper. Be prepared to explain your choice.

3. Review the conversation in Chapter 27 between the Roman, Flavius, and his Greek slave, Theodorus. Write a brief paragraph describing the viewpoint of Flavius about Greek culture. Be sure to include a topic sentence and details that back up the topic sentence.

Building Vocabulary Using Social Studies Terms

The passage below is adapted from *A History of the Ancient World* by Chester G. Starr. Read the passage. Write the numbers 1-10 on a sheet of paper. Match each numbered word or term in the passage with one of the definitions that follow. You may use your textbook, an encyclopedia, and a dictionary to check your choices. Use a dictionary that contains sections on biographical and geographical names.

The (1)Etruscans are one of the most fascinating and puzzling elements in all ancient history. From ancient times there has been a fierce debate on their origin. The Greek historian Dionysius of (2)Halicar-nassus considered them of native Italian origin. (3)Herodotus, on the other hand, recounted a tale of their movement from the (4)Aegean in a time of famine. Most modern scholars feel that both their strange language, which is not (5)Indo-European, and their strong ties with eastern customs support the view that they came from the east. It appears most probable that bands of Etruscans made their way west, perhaps from (6)Asia Minor. From the beginning the Etruscans seem to have organized themselves in the advanced (7)political form of the (8)city-state. Twelve of these states were united in a religious (9)league, but otherwise each state was absolutely independent. At first under kings and then under the leadership of the (10)aristocrats, the Etruscans spread their power rapidly and extensively.

a. nobles, members of a privileged class

b. sea between Asia Minor and Greece

c. peninsula of western Asia between the Black Sea and the Mediterranean Sea

d. independent state consisting of a city and surrounding territory

e. association of people or groups with a common interest

f. relating to the group of languages spoken by most Europeans and people of Iran and India

g. Greek historian who lived in the fifth century B.C.

h. ancient people who settled on the Italian peninsula

i. ancient city in Caria, on the southwest coast of Asia Minor

j. relating to a government

177

PART
6

THE ROMAN EMPIRE

I found Rome a city of bricks. I left it a city of marble."

This boast was made by Rome's first emperor, Octavian (ak-TAY-vee-un), who ruled Rome from 27 B.C. to 14 A.D. Octavian did give Rome many beautiful buildings worthy of the capital of a great empire. He also gave Romans something they had not had for a long time — peace and good government. A grateful Senate honored him with the title of Augustus. It meant that he stood above all other men.

Octavian (Augustus) created a civil service that was highly efficient. It enabled the empire to endure even the rule of an occasional madman like Nero (54-68 A.D.).

Fortunately for Rome, it had a number of very able emperors from the time of Augustus until about 200 years later. During this time towns and cities grew and prospered in every part of the empire. Excellent roads, bridges, and harbors were built to promote trade. Travelers could go quickly and safely from one end of the empire to another. Farmers raised food for all the people. Roman armies protected the empire's borders from invaders.

This period of peace and prosperity within the empire is often called the Pax Romana or Roman Peace. Edward Gibbon, a great historian who lived in the eighteenth century, had high praise for the Pax Romana. He called it "possibly the only period in which the happiness of a great people was the sole object of government."

The great days of the Pax Romana came to an end late in the second century A.D. At that time, a long decline began that was only temporarily checked by strong rulers. The emperor Diocletian (dy-uh-KLEE-shun) (284-305 A.D.) tried to "freeze" Roman society by introducing a *caste* system. It meant that sons had to follow in their fathers' trades. A soldier's son, for example, had to become a soldier.

To keep up the supply of food, peasants were bound to the soil. They could not leave the large estates on which they worked. Diocletian doubled the size of the army and taxed everyone to pay for it. His "reforms" made the Roman state more oppressive.

Another strong emperor, Constantine (CON-stan-teen), converted to Christianity in 312 A.D. and made it the official religion of the empire. He transferred the capital from Rome to a great city that he built close to Asia Minor (modern Turkey). He named it Constantinople, which means "city of Constantine." (Today it is known as Istanbul.)

In the fifth century A.D., the empire was invaded by Germanic tribes and a Mongol people called the Huns. Eventually the western half of the empire was overrun and destroyed. The eastern half of the empire, whose capital was Constantinople, survived the invasions and lasted another 1000 years.

What caused the downfall of the Roman empire in the west? Historians have offered many reasons for it. Among them are the following.

1. Augustus, Rome's first emperor, did not provide an orderly system of choosing a new emperor. During most of the third century A.D., the army picked the emperors. It usually chose generals who had no ability to run the government. The army often murdered emperors who displeased it.

2. The Roman state was bled by the ever-increasing demands of military adventurers.

3. A sharp drop in trade in the West caused its cities to decay.

4. Jobless workers in the cities used up public money.

5. Less food was produced due to poor farming methods on the large estates.

6. Epidemics of the plague and malaria killed about a third of the people.

Although the Roman Empire in the west was destroyed 1500 years ago, its civilization still influences the modern world. Some of the ways follow.

Roman law. The Romans developed good laws to settle disputes. Today Roman law is the basis of legal systems in much of Europe and Latin America.

The Latin language and writing. The Romans spoke and wrote Latin. Several languages of today stem from it. The main ones are Italian, French, Spanish, Portuguese, and Rumanian. Roman writers and poets are still read and admired by many people.

Buildings, roads, and bridges. The Romans were superb builders and engineers. Some of their roads, aqueducts, and public buildings are still used today. New buildings are made in the Roman style even now. Modern sports stadiums look very much like the Roman Colosseum.

Peace and unity. The Roman Empire united many different countries and people for a long time. The vision of a united, peaceful world still has a strong appeal.

29
The First Emperor

The year: 27 B.C.

The scene: the Roman Senate.

The action: Octavian, Caesar's adopted son, is about to make a speech.

It was all arranged in advance, very carefully. Some senators already knew what Octavian was going to say. Octavian had told them. He could count on their support. The others would surely follow their lead.

Now Octavian got up to speak. He stood near the spot where Julius Caesar had been murdered 17 years before. Some of the senators who had plotted the murder were present. But murder was not in their hearts this day. They did not care that now Octavian ruled almost as a king. His power was even greater than Caesar's. The Senate and the Roman people cared only about this: After 100 years of bloody civil wars, Octavian had brought peace back to Rome.

Romans were grateful to him that their lives and property were safe again. They wanted him to be their ruler, and Octavian knew it. He too believed that Rome needed a supreme ruler to keep peace and order. But he did not want to make the same mistake as Caesar. Caesar had looked down on the Senate and made many enemies there. Octavian would be smarter.

So Octavian began his speech to the Senate. He told the senators that he no longer wished to rule Rome. He wanted to be just like many of the old Roman heroes. They had become dictators to

Rome's first emperor, Augustus (above), brought peace to his people. Page 178: The story of another emperor, Trajan, is sculpted on a column. He leads troops from a city wall (base) and plans a city's defense (second level).

save Rome in times of danger. But as soon as the danger had passed, they gave their power back to the Senate. This, Octavian said, was what he wanted to do. He was going to retire and live as a private citizen. Rome, he said, could now become a republic again, ruled by the Senate.

Some senators knew that Octavian's speech was just a put-on. But most senators were shocked. They feared that they could not rule Rome anymore. Rome had become too big for them. When Rome was a small city-state, the Senate could manage it easily. But now Rome was the head of a great empire. It ruled 100 million people of many different nations, religions, and races. The Senate had not been able to keep peace in Italy. How could it keep peace in the whole empire? A strong man with great powers was needed to rule Rome now. Octavian could not retire.

Octavian "Gives In." The senators began to shout that Rome *needed* a king. This was just what Octavian wanted. Caesar had made the Senate angry by taking power against its will. Now the Senate was almost begging Octavian to be king.

Octavian then agreed to stay in power. However, he was a very clever man. He knew that many Romans still admired the old republic. They would not like the idea of a king with complete power. So Octavian let the Senate rule some parts

This carving shows the family of Emperor Augustus marching in a procession in Rome.

of the empire. But he kept control of the army, which meant that he had the upper hand. Octavian did not even call himself a king. Instead, he used other titles that gave him all the power he needed. One of these titles was Augustus. It meant that Octavian was not quite a god but was above all other men.

Octavian was soon called Augustus by all Romans. As the first Roman emperor, he ruled wisely for many years. He gave to all the people of the empire a just and honest government. Above all, he brought peace and order. Trade and business grew. Life became better for most people. A Greek writer praised Augustus with these words:

"Augustus has won for us a great peace. There are neither wars nor battles, robbers nor pirates. We may travel safely at all times from one end of the empire to the other."

While Augustus lived, many people in the empire believed he was a god. When he died in 14 A.D., the Roman Senate officially made him a god of the state.

✎ Quick Check

1. *How did Octavian get the support of the Senate? Why did his scheme work at that time in history?*

2. *What was Octavian's compromise with the Senate? What did Octavian control?*

3. *What did Octavian call himself? What did it mean?*

4. *How long did Octavian rule? Describe government, business, and the general atmosphere under his rule.*

30
Daily Life in Rome

How did the people of ancient Rome live? Even by modern standards, some of them had very lavish lifestyles. For those who could afford it, there was every luxury.

During the 200-years known as the Pax Romana, Rome had many good rulers and a prosperous empire. It lasted from 27 B.C. to 180 A.D. Many Romans lived in splendor. They ate rare foods like peacocks and larks' tongues at daily feasts. When they went out, they were carried in soft chairs by slaves. Women wore clothes of imported silk, perfume, and makeup. They were laden with jewelry. These things were only for the rich. However, even the poorest people enjoyed luxuries and entertainment.

Social Bathing. One of the good rulers of the Pax Romana was the emperor Trajan (TRAY-jan). He ruled from 98 to 117. During that period, bathing was a social custom that everyone, rich and poor, enjoyed. People went to big public bathhouses in the afternoons. The Romans were some of the cleanest people in history.

Roman baths were in big stone buildings. Sometimes they were surrounded with gardens. When people went to bathe, they first paid a small admission fee and then undressed. Men took off their *togas* (TOE-guz), garments that all free men had to wear. Togas were big pieces of woolen cloth carefully draped over one shoulder. They were usually

This detail from a fresco shows a wealthy Roman woman playing a cithara, an ancient kind of harp. The employment of slaves gave rich Romans time to pursue music and other arts. Note the woman's high-backed chair, a symbol of her upperclass status.

white, but some had bright-colored borders. Women took off their *pallas* (PAL-luz) which were thin wool capes. Both sexes wore long, colored tunics underneath.

After undressing, people exercised. Some of them wrestled. There were also many games played with balls, hoops, and other equipment. When they grew tired, they went into a hot, steamy room to sweat. This was followed by a hot bath, a cold bath, and then a swim. While rich and poor people bathed together, you could tell who was rich because they had slaves to scrub them. In some bathhouses, men and women bathed together. However, many Romans found this immodest. Eventually, bathhouses began to keep separate hours for women and men.

Gruesome Entertainment. After bathing, if it was a holiday, there might be free entertainment at the Colosseum (kahl-uh-SEE-um). This was a huge, round stadium that was open to the sky. Most of the entertainment there was horrifying by modern standards. Armed men and women called gladiators fought fierce animals such as lions and tigers. They would also fight each other to the death. Sometimes the fights were made to resemble sea battles. The floor of the Colosseum was flooded, and the gladiators were set afloat in small ships. Thou-

Powerful gladiators entertained Romans by fighting animals such as lions and tigers (below). When gladiators fought each other, they battled to the death.

188

sands of people and animals died there each year. The people were mostly criminals, prisoners of war, and others considered undesirable. So the Romans saw nothing wrong with this.

There was another ugly side to life in Rome. That was the slave system. Slaves were mostly people who were captured in wars. They were bought and sold as property. Some Romans treated their slaves with kindness. But many others treated them like work animals. Slaves were even kept chained by some owners. Owners had the right to kill their slaves for the slightest mistake. Sometimes a slave was punished unjustly. A slave once rebelled and killed his cruel master. The family of the dead man responded by killing the hundreds of slaves in the household.

Spartacus Leads Rebellion. In 73 B.C., a slave called Spartacus (SPAR-tuh-cuss) led a slave rebellion. He was a prisoner of war in training to be a gladiator. Spartacus managed to escape from gladiator school. He got together an army of 40,000 escaped slaves and frustrated peasants. The army terrorized southern Italy for two years, until they were beaten by the Roman army. Spartacus was crucified along with many of his soldiers.

The memory of Spartacus made many Romans just a little afraid of their slaves. The system was gradually reformed. The emperors Hadrian (HAY-dree-un) and Antoninus Pius (an-toe-NIHN-us PIE-us) introduced laws that made it illegal to kill or maim a slave. A Roman historian called Appian (APP-ee-uhn), who lived in the third century A.D., noted that in Rome it was hard to tell a slave from his master. Slaves were allowed to dress and act like citizens. If they were freed, they often became very important people.

Some historians, though, think that even with reforms, the slave system was bad for everyone. Romans forgot how to do anything for themselves. Even people who were not very wealthy had slaves to fulfill their every need. And free artisans and peasants were deprived of a way of making a living. Anything they could make or grow, a slave could do cheaper.

The Romans had created a culture of beauty and wealth unsurpassed by any previous culture. But underneath everything lay the seeds of decay. Great as the empire was, it could not last.

✎ Quick Check

1. *What was the Pax Romana, and to what period of time does it refer?*

2. *Why were the Romans among the cleanest people in history? What did typical Roman men and women wear?*

3. *What took place in the Colosseum? Who were the entertainers?*

4. *Who was Spartacus, and what did he do? When? What happened to him and his followers?*

5. *How did the conditions of slavery change over time? Give two reasons why slavery was bad for the Romans.*

31
The Roman Peace

The scene: a busy town in Gaul.

The year: 125 A.D.

The action: two pottery makers are having lunch.

JULIUS: Have you heard the news, Valerius (va-LAIR-ee-us)? Emperor Hadrian is planning a big outdoor theater for our town. Think of it! Soon actors, singers, and dancers will put on shows for us. Our town is really getting up in the world. A few years ago, the emperor gave us a stadium. Before that, he built our public baths. Yes, the Romans have been good to us, Valerius.

VALERIUS: You are forgetting one important thing, Julius. Before the Romans came, our people were free from outside rule. We made our own rules. We did not take orders from a Roman governor. When we were free, we stood up and did things for ourselves. Now we depend on the Romans for everything. And we imitate all their ways. We speak *their* language, Latin, instead of our own. We use Latin names, instead of the names of Gaul. The Romans build temples to *their* deities, and we worship in them. We have become like children. We are well fed, but we do as we are told.

JULIUS: I am amazed to hear you talk that

way, Valerius. Roman rule is not hard at all. All we must do is pay our taxes and be loyal to the emperor. In return, the Romans give us peace and protection from robbers and pirates. It is safe to travel anywhere on land or sea. You don't have to worry about being kidnapped and sold as a slave. And travel is fast. You can easily ride a horse 100 miles a day on Roman roads. Roads connect all our cities and are as straight as arrows. A letter mailed to Rome will get there by ship in 10 days. Is it any wonder that trade and business are so good? Aren't we living much better than our grandfathers? Look at this meal we are eating, with fine olives and good wine. Who taught us to plant olive trees and grape vines? The Romans!

VALERIUS: Well, Julius, maybe our grandfathers liked to herd cattle. And they didn't care about things such as business or travel or even olives. The important thing to them was that they were independent. Are we independent?

JULIUS: There you go again. It might be nice to be independent. But independence isn't worth anything unless you can enjoy it. The Romans treat us fairly. Their laws protect everyone. Why, even slaves are protected by Roman law. Suppose a slave is treated badly by his master. He has the right to protest to the Roman governor. The governor may then give him a kinder master, or even free him.

VALERIUS: All that is true, Julius. But tell me one thing. Do we Gauls have the same rights as Romans?

JULIUS: Many of us do, Valerius. Any Gaul who serves in the army or government of Rome becomes a Roman citizen. Then he has the same rights as any man born in Rome. He may become an army commander, a governor, a senator, or even emperor. That is true in almost every part of the empire. Surely you know that our great emperor Hadrian comes from Spain. Yes, if a man serves Rome well, Rome rewards him well. I would much rather live under Roman rule than be independent.

VALERIUS: That is a pity, Julius. Unfortunately, most Gauls agree with you.

✎ Quick Check

1. *What were some of the benefits of Roman rule in Gaul? What did the Romans expect in return?*

2. *According to Valerius, what happens to people if they lose their independence? What two Roman "imports" did he resent?*

3. *Could non-Romans become citizens? How? Who was a striking example of a non-Roman who rose to power?*

32
Jesus of Nazareth

Perhaps no figure in history has stirred the hearts and minds of people more than Jesus of Nazareth. Yet we know very little about his life. What was he like in his youth? Did he get along well with his parents? Was he playful or serious? What did he look like? These are questions that cannot be answered. All we know about Jesus comes from four very brief accounts of his life called the Gospels. They begin the New Testament of the Christian Bible. The Gospels tell us almost nothing about the childhood and youth of Jesus. They even leave doubt about the year of his birth. Two of the Gospels do not mention his birth at all. The Gospels of Matthew and Luke say that Jesus was born in Bethlehem. The date may have been anywhere from 4 B.C. to 8 A.D.

Humble Birth. According to Luke, the Roman Emperor Augustus (see chapter 29) ordered a *census*, or population count, to be taken in his empire. From the town of Nazareth, a carpenter named Joseph and his wife, Mary, traveled to Bethlehem to be counted. While they were there, Mary gave birth to her first son, Jesus. It happened in a stable because, Luke says, "There was no room for them at the inn."

Of the childhood of Jesus, only one story is told. Luke says that Jesus' parents, who were Jewish, went each year to Jerusalem to celebrate the feast of Passover. One year, when Jesus was 12, the parents began their journey home by caravan. They were unaware that Jesus had stayed behind in the city. When they realized that he was missing, they returned

This wall sculpture shows Mary and Joseph fleeing into Egypt with their son, Jesus, after the king of Judea ordered the infant killed.

to Jerusalem. After three days, they found him in the great temple. His mother scolded him for causing them so much worry. Jesus replied, "Why did you have to search for me? Did you not know that I was bound to be in my Father's house?"

Apart from this incident, we know only that Jesus grew up in Nazareth. Luke says that "The child grew and became strong, filled with wisdom, and the favor of God was upon him."

Jesus' Vision. The story of Jesus' life resumes when he is about 30 years old. At that time he began his calling as a religious teacher and prophet. It ended

193

with his tragic death no more than three years later. The writers of the Gospels focus on this period. For in that short time, Jesus began a movement that eventually would change the course of world history.

What led Jesus to his religious calling? The Gospels say that it began after he heard John the Baptist preach in the desert. John warned his listeners of a terrible day of judgment to come when God would punish the wicked. To save themselves, they must repent for their sins and live selflessly. Those who wished to repent were baptized by John in the Jordan River. Baptism was a rite of purification and cleansing. Impressed by John's message, Jesus was baptized. It was a tremendously moving experience for him. The Gospel author Mark describes its effect:

> At the moment when he came out of the water, Jesus saw the heavens open and the Spirit of God, like a dove, descending upon him. And a voice spoke from heaven: "Thou art my Son, my Beloved, and with thee I am well pleased."

At this moment, Jesus understood his mission. It was to preach God's word for the salvation of humanity.

When Jesus began to preach, his message was, "The kingdom of God is at hand. Repent, and believe the good news." To his listeners, the meaning of Jesus' words was quite clear. He was saying that the present, evil age was about to end. But he was not a prophet of doom. For those who would repent and do good, a wonderful new age was coming. For the poor and the downtrodden especially, Jesus' message had a strong appeal. They had nothing to lose and everything to gain by the end of the present world as it was.

Jesus' compassion for the lowly is eloquently expressed in his Sermon on the Mount. In it he said:

> Blessed are the poor, for theirs is the kingdom of heaven.
> Blessed are those who mourn, for they shall be comforted.
> Blessed are the meek, for they shall inherit the earth.
> Blessed are the merciful, for they shall obtain mercy.
> Blessed are the pure in heart, for they shall see God.
> Blessed are the peacemakers, for they shall be called the children of God.
> Blessed are those who are persecuted, for great is their reward in heaven.

MAP EXERCISE

According to the account of St. Luke, Joseph and Mary traveled from Nazareth to Bethlehem for a census. Use this map to answer the following questions:

1. In which direction did they travel? How far was their journey?

2. The Jordan River connects what two seas? Which of the three regions of Palestine bordered on the Mediterranean?

194

PALESTINE IN THE TIME OF JESUS

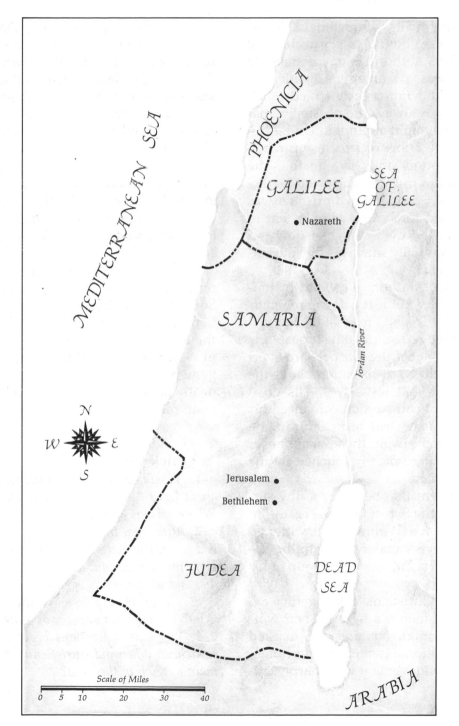

PHOENICIA

GALILEE

SEA OF GALILEE

● Nazareth

MEDITERRANEAN SEA

SAMARIA

Jordan River

N
W E
S

Jerusalem ●

Bethlehem ●

JUDEA

DEAD SEA

Scale of Miles

0   5   10   20   30   40

ARABIA

195

Popularity Brings Punishment. Jesus' teachings were bound to alarm the civil and religious authorities of his time. To some, he was a dangerous fanatic. Although he did not preach armed rebellion, there was always the possibility that his followers might attempt it. Under Roman law, the crime of stirring up rebellion was punishable by death. The Roman method of execution was particularly brutal. A condemned prisoner was nailed or tied to a cross. He was left to dangle until he died of exhaustion and hunger. Eventually such was the fate suffered by Jesus.

The Gospel authors were not historians but men of faith. It was the religious meaning of Jesus' life that concerned them, not the recording of historical facts and events. But if the Gospels are short on history, they tell us much about the kind of man that Jesus was. His great goodness and compassion convinced his followers that he had been sent among them by God. Even those who never knew Jesus were deeply touched by the story of his life.

A movement that began as a tiny stirring around the Sea of Galilee became an irresistable force. Within 20 years after Jesus' death, every major center in the Roman Empire had at least one group of his followers.

The early Christians met together every day in someone's house. Their worship was spontaneous and was marked by great emotional excitement. In Rome, the Christian movement was sharply criticized in the popular press. One writer said, "The Christians form among themselves secret societies that exist outside the system of laws....Their alliance consists in meetings at night with solemn rituals and inhuman revelries....They despise temples as if they were tombs. They disparage the deities and ridicule our sacred rites. Like a growth of weeds, the haunts where they meet are multiplying all over the world....These depraved wretches revere an executed criminal and the wooden cross on which he was executed."

Despite persecution, the Christian movement grew at an amazing rate. Soon it was no longer possible for Christians to meet informally. By the end of the first century A.D., worship took place in churches under the direction of clergymen. Within three centuries after the death of Jesus, Christianity became the main religion in the Western world.

✎ Quick Check

1. *Where does the information we have about Jesus come from? Where was he born? Where was his family from?*

2. *After what incident did Jesus feel that he had to preach God's word? How old was he? How many years did he preach? How did he die, and what was his offense?*

3. *To whom did Jesus' teaching appeal? Why? Who did not approve of Jesus? Why?*

4. *When did Christians begin to meet in churches? When did Christianity become the main religion in the West?*

196

33
A Challenge to the Emperors

In the Roman Empire, there were many religions. Many people worshipped the household deities of the early Romans. Others worshipped Greek or even Egyptian deities. The Roman government didn't mind. It did object, though, to the worship of the Christians. Why? Christians would not worship Rome's emperors as gods. Many of them would not serve in the Roman army or government. Some emperors tried to force Christians to give up their beliefs. Many Christians who refused were put in jail, or even killed.

The year: 250 A.D.

The scene: the home of Marcellus (mar-SELL-us), a Roman merchant.

The action: Marcellus and his friend, Titus (TIE-tus), are having dinner.

TITUS: Well, Marcellus, it looks like Emperor Decius (DEE-shuss) is cracking down on the Christians. He says that they must swear loyalty to the deities of Rome. If they do, they will be all right. But if they refuse, they will be put in jail. They will get no food or water until they change their minds. What do you think of that?

MARCELLUS: I'm all for it, Titus. I say it's about time we stopped babying those Christians. Our courts have been much too easy on them. Most of our judges actually seem to protect them. What happens when someone is accused of being a Christian? First, the judge demands all kinds of proof that it is true. Well, it's hard to prove that someone is a Christian, Titus. You know that. Those people are very

197

Underground cemeteries, or catacombs, like this one were built by early Christians. The catacombs provided them with secret places for worship.

clever. They have their meetings in secret, usually at night.

So what does the judge do? He throws the case out of court. Or he finds some other excuse to let the person off easy. The person is sent to work in the mines or goes to jail. Six months later, he or she is pardoned and then is free again.

I tell you, Titus, we have to get tough with those people. I say we should put them all in jail and throw away the key. Or better yet, throw them to the lions. That's what some governors do at times. It's really the best way.

TITUS: Tell me, Marcellus, why are you so bitter about these Christians? I have a number of Christian friends, and they are really very good people. In many

198

ways, they behave much better than the average Roman. Most Romans today seem to care only about pleasure. They want to be amused constantly by festivals and games. But these Christians are different. They don't care much about money, and they are content to live simply. They are good family people—they don't drink or carry on at night. Above all, they want so much to do good. They try to outdo each other with kindness and patience and modesty. Surely, Marcellus, such people do not deserve the kind of treatment you're suggesting.

MARCELLUS: Titus, you amaze me. I never thought I would hear a friend of mine defend Christians! Don't you understand that these people are enemies of the state? They refuse to admit that our Roman emperors are gods. They predict that the Roman Empire will come to an end. They say that the kingdom of heaven will take its place! Many refuse to serve in the army or the government. What would become of our empire if every man refused to become a soldier? Right now, Marcellus, the German barbarians are attacking our borders. The empire is in great danger. And any man who will not fight is a traitor!

TITUS: The empire must be defended, of course. But let's be honest, Marcellus. How many Romans serve in the army these days? More and more we are hiring soldiers from outside Italy to fight for us. Besides, how many Christians

are there? Maybe one person out of 20 in our empire is a Christian. There just aren't enough Christians to help us much in our defense.

MARCELLUS: True, but the number of Christians keeps growing. They are such stubborn people. They never stop preaching about Jesus. They say that they must be loyal to him, rather than our emperors. And who was this Jesus? I hear that he was the son of a poor Jewish carpenter. How can they call a beggar like that the Son of God?

TITUS: I'm sure I don't know, Marcellus. In our empire people worship many different deities. And we Romans have usually permitted them to worship as they please. Should we not also permit the Christians to worship as they please?

MARCELLUS: Do not compare the Christians with other people in our empire! Other people have their own deities, it is true. But they also respect our emperor as a god and other Roman deities. The Christians say that all our deities are really evil spirits! For this they must be severely punished.

✎ Quick Check

1. *Of what crime were the Christians guilty according to Roman law? How were they punished?*

2. *About what percent of Romans were Christians in the third century?*

3. *In what ways were the Christians good members of society? In what ways did other Romans consider them bad?*

34
The Visigoths: A Threat to Rome

A tribe of Visigoths (VIZ-ih-goths) was eating supper. They had hunted and killed a wild boar. They were good hunters because they were strong and hardy. Although they had warm woolen clothing, they sometimes wore only a few animal skins. They believed that being cold would make them tough.

A group of people from another tribe appeared. True to the Germanic ideal of hospitality, they were invited to stay for supper. After everyone had eaten, both tribes began to talk about their leaders. Each claimed that their leader was the best.

A young man from the first tribe said, "Our leader is a great warrior. He fights with all his strength and risks his life to save ours. It would be shameful to die before him in battle. With him as our leader, we almost always win. He has helped us take many things from Roman cities. And he has protected us against the fierce Huns."

A woman from the second tribe said, "Our leader is very just. He shares the wealth from our victories fairly. People get rewards that are large or small according to how brave they were. But our leader is careful to see that nobody has too much or too little."

A third person said, "Our leader is very pious. While many are converting to Christianity, he follows the good old ways. Yesterday he sacrificed five goats to the war god Tiwaz and fertility goddess Nerthus."

Who were these people? They were nomads from Germany who dared to challenge the Romans. They wanted to

An influx of Visigoths weakened the Roman Empire. As in this sculpture, Roman soldiers often dealt with barbarian prisoners by cutting off their heads.

live on Roman land, but the Romans wanted to keep them out. The Romans found them rough and uncivilized. They called them barbarians. Yet, they also secretly admired them for their courage and simple ways of living.

One of the most important Germanic tribes were called Visigoths. They came from southern Sweden in about 200 A.D. From there they slowly moved south through Germany. In 375 A.D., they were attacked by the warrior Huns of Asia. To protect themselves, the Visigoths crossed the Danube River near the Black Sea. Then they were inside the Roman Empire.

Value Strength and Loyalty. The Visigoths lived in small tribes, loosely united by their king. Each tribe was headed by a leader. Tribal order was based on loyalty to a strong leader. This was also true of many other Germanic tribes. They included the Saxons, the Lombards, and the Vandals.

These people did not live in comfortable houses. They built small homes out of wood, and they often lived in them for less than a year. Unlike the Romans, they did not want many possessions. A person's worth was based on bravery rather than wealth. They did not even have a system of money. Instead, they used Roman coins and cattle as currency.

The tribes had a few simple laws. If someone was harmed or robbed, the guilty person would have to pay a fine. Guilt was determined by a test. The accused person might be made to walk on fire. If the wounds healed quickly, the person was declared innocent. If they didn't, the person was considered guilty. This was called *trial by ordeal*.

Tribal Life. Like the Romans, the Germanic tribes worshipped many gods and goddesses. The most important ones were Tiwaz and Nerthus. They worshipped them in sacred groves of oak trees, instead of temples. Sometimes humans and animals were sacrificed there. Rituals to predict the future were also performed. Although tribes had a written language, it was mainly used to keep track of religious rituals. Occasionally someone wrote down the recipe for a potion or a medicine.

The tribes ate mostly what they could hunt and gather in the woods. They grew a little grain and got milk from their

MAP EXERCISE

This map shows the paths taken by invaders of the Roman Empire. Use it and a map of modern Europe to answer the following:

1. What non-Germanic invaders came from the Far East?

2. Where did the Saxons come from? Where did they go? What other group came from the same area as the Saxons?

3. What group of invaders came from what is now Sweden?

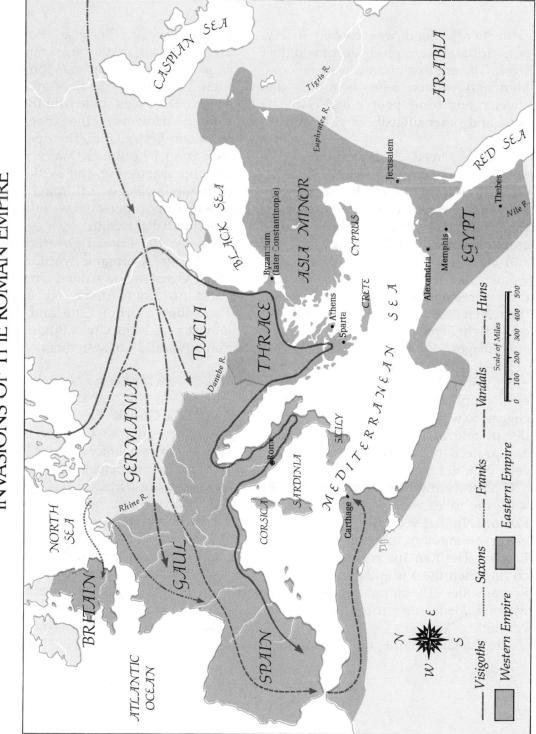

INVASIONS OF THE ROMAN EMPIRE

CASPIAN SEA

ARABIA

Tigris R.

Euphrates R.

RED SEA

Jerusalem

Thebes

Nile R.

EGYPT

Memphis

Alexandria

BLACK SEA

Byzantium
(later Constantinople)

ASIA MINOR

CYPRUS

CRETE

DACIA

THRACE

Athens

Sparta

MEDITERRANEAN SEA

Danube R.

Huns

Vandals

Scale of Miles

0   100   200   300   400   500

GERMANIA

SICILY

Rome

SARDINIA

Franks

NORTH
SEA

Rhine R.

CORSICA

Carthage

Saxons

Eastern Empire

BRITAIN

GAUL

SPAIN

ATLANTIC
OCEAN

N
W   E
S

Visigoths

Western Empire

cattle herds. Food was cooked in clay pots. Tribal artisans rarely decorated their work. The one exception was metalwork. Men and women wore beautiful gold jewelry, and some people had elaborate cups and other utensils of gold and silver.

Women played an important role in domestic, political, and spiritual life. Because men were constantly away in battle, women were in charge of keeping the tribe fed and clothed. They planted crops, cooked, washed, brewed beer, and cared for the sick. In some tribes, women had political influence. Because they were considered physically weaker than men, they did not go to war, but could fight fiercely to defend their homes and villages.

Tribal women were believed to have great spiritual strength. They were powerful prophets and priestesses and gave charms to warriors to bring victory in battle. In return, they were given respect and protection. This was part of the tribal code of honor.

Overpowering the Romans. By 376 A.D., the tribes were a real threat to the Romans. In that year, the Visigoths were given permission to enter the Roman Empire. The Romans regretted their decision when the Visigoths began to sack Roman cities. They grew more and more worried about other tribes invading the empire.

The Roman Empire and its armies had become weak. Because Romans no longer served in the army, the eastern emperor, Theodosius, was forced to hire some Visigoths as soldiers. As payment, he gave the tribes some land that nobody wanted. However, the tribes wanted more and better land. Their people were increasing in number. Many wanted to give up wandering and settle down in permanent villages. Although they still frowned upon personal wealth, they believed in tribal wealth.

Finally, the Roman government even had to hire Germanic warriors to fight other Germanic warriors! The Romans could no longer defend their borders. The tribes overran Gaul and began to move towards the city of Rome itself. The Romans could not stop them.

✎ Quick Check

1. *Where did the Visigoths come from? Why and when did they cross the Danube and enter the Roman Empire? Name at least two other Germanic tribes.*

2. *What was trial by ordeal? On what was a Visigoth's worth based?*

3. *Describe Visigoth houses, places of worship, religion, and system of government.*

4. *What did women contribute to daily tribal life? What special power were they supposed to have? What did they get in return?*

5. *What was Theodosius forced to do? What were the consequences?*

35
City of Constantine

Some Roman emperors tried very hard to make the empire stronger. One of them was Constantine. He became a Christian and gave Christians the right to worship freely. Constantine was an important emperor in other ways. Because of a decision he made, part of the Roman Empire lasted for almost 1000 years after Rome was captured by Germanic tribes.

Emperor Constantine was in trouble. The people of Rome wanted to know if he worshipped their deities. A Roman emperor was expected to.

Constantine was not liked in Rome. He was an outsider. He came from an area of the empire known today as Yugoslavia (you-go-SLAV-ee-uh). Constantine chose to rule the empire from cities in the East. The people of Rome said that he had turned his back on them.

Constantine had made the Romans angry in other ways. Most of them still believed in the old Roman deities. But Constantine had become a Christian. He had given Christians the right to worship freely. Now he was giving money to build great churches in Rome. He had even chosen a Christian governor for the city. The Roman Senate and the people did not like it at all.

Now, in 326 A.D., Constantine was visiting Rome. He had come back to cele-

brate an important event. It was 20 years since he had become emperor. On this day, the soldiers were lined up for a parade. They were going to march with their emperor to the great temple of Jupiter (JOO-pih-ter). Jupiter was the chief god of Rome. But Constantine refused to march in a pagan parade.

The people and the senators began to curse Constantine. A riot almost broke out, but the soldiers kept order. They were still loyal to their emperor.

A Capital Solution. Constantine had never liked Rome. Now he liked it even less. He began to think about building a new capital city for the empire. He wanted this city to be in the East, close to Asia Minor. He had several reasons:

▪ The towns and farms of the East were rich. The East had not suffered as much damage as the West from the attacks of the Germanic tribes.

▪ The best soldiers in the empire now came from the East. Some of these soldiers, like Constantine, had become Roman emperors. A city in the East would be good for the defense of the empire.

▪ The East had many more Christians than the West. Christianity had started in the eastern part of the empire. Constantine knew that the Christians would support him.

Constantine finally chose an old Greek city called Byzantium (bih-ZAN-she-um). Only a very narrow piece of water separated it from Asia Minor. Constantine began to rebuild the city. Workers came from all over the empire to do the job. Constantine wanted his new capital to be as great as Rome. He did not care how much it cost. New taxes would take care of that.

The new capital soon began to look much like Rome. The Great Palace of Constantine was built next to a big racetrack. Constantine could watch the races from his palace windows. The forum was paved with marble. A golden statue of Constantine stood on a high column in the center. The sidewalks of the main avenue were decorated with hundreds of bronze statues. Most of them were stolen by Constantine's agents from cities in Greece. The public baths were in a big building with walls of marble. Constantine also built a fine church.

Constantinople's Birthday. Constantine named his new capital after himself. He called it Constantinople (con-stan-tih-NO-pel) — the city of Constantine. The city was ready on May 11, 330. There were parades, feasts, and games for the next 40 days. Both Christian and pagan priests prayed for Constantine. To many people, he was a god like emperors used to be.

At the racetrack, soldiers had a parade in his honor. They wore their best uni-

Constantine, the first Roman emperor to become a Christian, made Christianity legal. In this painting he leads a Christian pope into Rome.

forms and held white candles in their hands. Some guarded a golden statue of Constantine that was carried in a wagon. The people bowed down to the statue and praised the emperor. When the statue came to Constantine, he saluted it. Then he ordered the same parade to be held on each birthday of the city.

What made Constantinople so important? After Constantine died, the Roman Empire split in two. The western half was ruled by one emperor in Rome. The eastern half was ruled by another emperor in Constantinople. Tribes soon overran the western empire, but the eastern empire held them off. It lasted more than 1000 years. The laws, arts, and sci-ences of Rome and Greece lived on in the eastern Roman Empire.

✎ Quick Check

1. *What was Constantine's major disagreement with the people of Rome?*

2. *Why did Constantine build a new capital in the East? What city was located on the site he chose? Where was it? What did he name the new city?*

3. *When was the new capital completed? Briefly describe it.*

4. *How did Constantine pay for such a splendid city? Where did he get some of the statues that decorated its avenues? What did people in the East think of Constantine? What happened to the Roman Empire after he died?*

36
The Fall of Rome

The people of Rome were in a panic. A large army of Visigoths had crossed the Alps and entered Italy. The Visigoths spread terror in the northern cities by stealing everything they could carry away. Now, in 410 A.D., they were marching on Rome. And the city was helpless. It had no defense at all against invaders.

The Romans had changed a lot since the early days when they won a great empire. The wealthy senators and nobles had grown soft and lazy. Some writers and critics were disgusted by the extreme luxury in which many people lived. The Roman historian Ammianus (ahm-ih-AY-nuss) wrote that a noble person would not even swat a fly but, instead, waited for a slave to do it. They would not fight in the army or send their sons to fight.

What about the common people? Most of the tough farmers of Italy had lost their land to larger, richer farms. Rome was filled with thousands of people who had no jobs. Many were freed slaves and drifters from all over the empire. They could not find jobs because slaves did most of the work. They lived in dark and crowded slums. The emperor kept them quiet by giving them free bread, pork, oil, and cheap wine every month. He also entertained them with free gladiator fights and chariot races. Most of the drifters loafed in the streets and gambled all day. They were lazy and no use as soldiers.

Visigoth Siege. Where was the young emperor Honorius (hah-NOR-ee-us) while the Visigoths were marching on Rome? He had fled to the safety of Rav-

enna, which was a long way from Rome. Honorius had actually left a Vandal soldier in charge of the Roman government. This soldier, Stilicho (STILL-ih-koh), had kept the Visigoths away from Rome seven years earlier. However, the Roman Senate began to suspect Stilicho of plotting to murder Honorius. Honorius ordered Stilicho executed. Consequently, there was no one in charge of Rome in 410. It was easy for the Visigoth king Alaric (AL-ah-rick) and his army to march on Rome.

Alaric's army did not try to break into Rome at once. The city was protected by strong, high walls. Instead, the army surrounded Rome and did not let any food in. This was a *siege*. Soon the Romans were starving. The rich spent their money on the food that was left. The poor ate anything they could find, even rats. It was rumored that some desperate people killed and ate other people. Thousands of people died of hunger, and there was no place to bury them. Then disease spread over the city, and more people died.

Frightened, the Senate decided to talk to Alaric. First they tried to threaten him. They pretended that they had a large army waiting inside the city walls. Alaric just laughed. He knew that the Romans were really desperate.

At last, Alaric offered to stop the siege in return for some treasure. He asked for 5000 pounds of gold and 3000 pounds of costly pepper, among other things. The senators asked him, "O king, if these are your demands, what do you plan to leave us with?" "Your lives!" thundered the proud king.

Alaric was true to his word. Although he burned many of the great mansions of Rome, all Romans who did not fight back were spared. The great public buildings were left standing. Alaric was especially careful to leave the churches alone, because he considered himself a Christian.

An Easy Target. The Romans tried to resume life as usual after Alaric and his army finally left. But their spirit was broken. They had been humbled by the very people they had looked down upon. Their government was in chaos. In 455, a second Germanic tribe called the Vandals sacked Rome. They took pleasure in destroying many of the buildings that Alaric had spared. The meaning of the word *vandal* comes from their conduct.

Finally, a Germanic king called Odoacer (oh-doh-AY-sir) attacked Rome for the third time in 476. He proclaimed himself emperor of the western empire. Tribal kings and chiefs now ruled all of Western Europe. The Roman Empire in the West was dead.

✎ Quick Check

1. *Give two reasons why the western part of the Roman Empire collapsed. What did the emperor do during the first wave of invasions? Identify Stilicho.*

2. *Who was Alaric, and how did he conquer Rome? How did he treat the conquered city?*

3. *Where does the word* vandal *come from? What king lead the final invasion of Rome?*

PART 6
Review and Skills Exercises

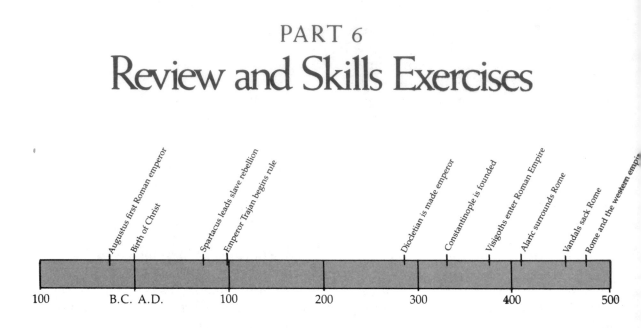

Understanding Events

In the few centuries covered in Part 6, the Roman Empire grew tremendously. But the last 100 years were marked by a shift in the capital from Rome to Constantinople and the crumbling of the western part. Study the time line above and answer the following questions.

1. The rule of Augustus began a period known as the Roman Peace. When did it begin?

2. When did the Roman Empire in the West come to an end?

3. What is the relationship between the birth of Christ and the way we reckon time?

4. Who founded Constantinople? What connection did he have with the religion founded by the followers of Jesus?

5. When did the Visigoths enter the Roman Empire? What was the outcome of the invasion of the Roman Empire by the Germanic tribes?

Expressing a Point of View

Chapter 31 contains a conversation between two men in Gaul in 125 A.D. Gaul, most of which is now modern-day France, was conquered by the Roman emperor Julius Caesar in 51 B.C. and remained under Roman rule for 300 years. In the conversation, the two men express different points of view, or different ways of thinking, about life under the Romans. The two statements below sum up the opposing points of view of the two men. Read the statements and answer the questions that follow.

Julius argues that peace, protection, and a good life are most important for a society. And that's what the Romans brought to Gaul. We now have a stadium, a theater, public baths, fine foods, and safety from pirates and robbers. What more could anyone want?

Valerius argues that doing things on your own is what counts most. Even if you have to struggle, you're still your own man. Most Gauls may be well fed, but they have to do as they are told by the Romans. They're no better off than children.

1. Why does Julius think life under Roman rule is good?

2. What does Valerius object to about life under Roman rule?

3. Do you agree with Julius or with Valerius? Do you agree partly with one and partly with the other? Write a brief explanation of why you made your choice.

4. What is your reaction to Julius's opinion that protection and safety are important? Consider this point: Our society has traffic rules to protect citizens. An individual cannot drive anywhere and in any manner he or she wants. Can you think of some other types of laws that require individuals to give up some freedom for the good of all?

Building Vocabulary

Write the numbers 1-7 on a sheet of paper to correspond to the numbered sentences below. By each number write the words from the list that best complete each sentence.

1. The Roman ruler Octavian succeeded in getting the _____ to declare him _____ with the title _____.

2. A long period of peace in the Roman Empire is known as the _____.

3. During Roman times, _____ might be the death penalty for the crime of _____, or inciting a rebellion.

4. In Rome a huge stadium called the _____ was the scene of spectacles such as _____ doing battle with wild animals.

5. The _____ and the _____ were two of the Germanic tribes that attacked the Roman Empire in the fourth and fifth centuries A.D.

6. Modern-day France was known as _____ in Roman times.

7. The Romans called the Germanic peoples _____, a term early Greeks used to describe those who were not Greek.

emperor	Augustus
barbarians	Gaul
Visigoths	Vandals
Colosseum	gladiators
crucifixion	sedition
Pax Romana	Roman Senate

GLOSSARY

A.D. abbreviation for *anno Domini* that refers to dates within the Christian era.

agriculture. the practice of producing crops and raising livestock.

alliance. a joining together of groups to promote their mutual interests.

aqueduct. a channel that carried fresh water to a city or town.

archaeology. the study of cultures through their remains such as tools, weapons, pottery, buildings, and writings.

architecture. the design of buildings.

artisan. a trained or skilled worker; a craftsworker.

assembly. a meeting of people for a specific purpose; often, a group of people who make laws.

B.C. an abbreviation for *before Christ* indicating the period of time occurring before the Christian era.

baptism. a Christian ritual in which water symbolizes the admittance of an individual into the Christian community.

barbarians. a term used to describe uncivilized people. The Greeks used this word to describe all non-Greeks.

battering ram. a large wooden beam with an iron tip. It was used to break down walls during a battle.

caravan. a group of vehicles, such as wagons, traveling together, often through a desert.

caste system. a social system in which people are ranked according to their occupation, wealth, family, religion, or some other characteristic.

catapult. a military device that was used to hurl spears and stones.

centaur. a creature from Greek mythology that was half man, half horse.

chariot. a two wheeled vehicle drawn by horses that was used in sports, processions, and battles.

citizen. a person who owes loyalty to a government and in return receives rights, privileges, and protection.

city. a densely populated area that usually does not produce all its own food and lives by trade.

city-state. an independent community made up of a city and the surrounding area.

civilization. a level of cultural development that involves food production, some sort of central government, permanent buildings, and sometimes a system of writing.

class. a grouping of people according to similar social and economic levels.

Code of Hammurabi. laws written by the Babylonian king Hammurabi. It was one of the first sets of laws used to govern a kingdom.

colony. a territory over which a nation claims the right of possession and has political and economic control.

consul. one of two annually elected chief officials of the Roman Republic.

covenant. a formal promise by a person or people to obey the laws of their deity.

crafts. arts or trades such as pottery-making, that require skill with the hands.

culture. the way that a certain group of people have adapted to their environment. A culture is defined by tools, customs, values, religion, food, and clothing.

cuneiform. a means of writing consisting of wedge-shaped elements. It was usually written in clay or stone.

deity. god or goddess.

delta. a strip of fertile land, usually triangular in shape, located at the mouth of a river.

democracy. a form of government in which the people either rule directly or through elected representatives.

dictator. a person who has absolute authority and unlimited power over a nation or a state.

dike. a structure used to control or confine water.

dowry. the money, goods, or land that a woman brings into a marriage.

economy. a system for making, distributing, and using goods and services.

empire. a state, territory, or group of states ruled by a single government.

environment. conditions such as weather and geography that influence the culture and development of a people.

ethical monotheism. the belief in one god combined with a commitment to morality and social justice.

Fertile Crescent. a crescent-shaped area of land in the Middle East that included parts of Mesopotamia, Phoenicia, and Canaan.

fortified. strengthened against invaders by surrounding walls, battle towers, etc.

fresco. a wall painting made by applying water-based coloring to wet plaster.

gladiator. a person trained to fight to death with other people or animals for the entertainment of the ancient Romans.

gymnasium. a large room used for indoor sports.

hieroglyphics. a type of writing that uses pictures or symbols that represent letters, words, ideas, or sounds.

history. the study of the past since the development of writing.

irrigation. a means of supplying farmland with water by building canals, dams, etc.

kingdom. an area ruled by a king or queen.

Marathon. the Greek town where the Greeks defeated the Persians in 490 B.C. The news of the victory was carried 26 miles to Athens by a runner.

merchant. a buyer, seller, and trader of goods for profit.

migration. the movement of people from one country or area to another.

monarchy. a government headed by a ruler such as a king, queen, emperor, or empress.

monotheism. the belief in one god.

mummy. a corpse preserved by treating it with salt and spices and wrapping it in cloth.

myth. a popular story, belief, or tradition that has grown up around something or someone. Myths were the backbone of early Greek paganism.

nation. a group of people united into a large political, economic, and social unit.

nomad. a member of a group that has no permanent town or village but wanders from place to place.

nymphs. beautiful maidens who were minor deities in Greek mythology. They always lived outdoors.

oasis. a fertile area with a water supply surrounded by desert.

ode. a lyric poem usually devoted to praising someone or something.

orator. a person who is skilled at public speaking.

pagan. a person who worships more than one deity; a religion that has more than one deity.

papyrus. a reedy plant that the Egyptians used to make paper.

patricians. a class of wealthy landowners.

patriotism. a sense of loyalty to one's country and its ideals.

Pax Romana. a period of domestic peace in ancient Rome, which lasted from 27 B.C. to 180 B.C.

people, a. all the persons who belong to an ethnic group.

pentathlon. an athletic contest made up of five different events.

pharaoh. a ruler of ancient Egypt who was worshipped as a deity.

plateau. a flat piece of land that is higher than the surrounding land.

plebians. common people.

politics. the art and science of government. The competition between groups and individuals for power and leadership.

prehistory. the study of the past before the development of writing.

prophet. a wise and respected person who sometimes makes predictions about the future.

pyramid. a four-sided stone structure with a pointed top. In Egypt they were the tombs of the pharaohs and nobility.

reform. a change for the better.

republic. a government in which the rulers are not monarchs but are chosen by the people or some select group.

role. the part one plays in a social group.

Senate. the governing body of the Roman Republic and the Roman Empire.

siege. a military blockade of a city or town in order to force its people to surrender.

shekel. a silver coin used by the ancient Hebrews.

skilled. trained, having expert ability.

slave. a person who is owned by another person, either temporarily or permanently.

society. any group of people who have a shared culture or identity.

sphinx. an Egyptian statue with the head of a human being and the body of a lion. It usually represented the pharaoh.

surplus. more than is needed.

Ten Commandments. a set of 10 laws that were the foundation of the Hebrew faith. They stressed moral behavior and commitment to one God.

town. a settled area larger in size and population than a village but smaller than a city.

trade. buying, selling, or trading goods and services.

treaty. a formal agreement between two nations.

trial by ordeal. a test of guilt first used by Germanic tribespeople. A person accused of wrongdoing was forced into a dangerous situation or forced to endure bodily harm. If they survived or their injuries healed quickly, they were declared innocent.

tribe. a people who have the same language, religion, government and culture, and who are united under one leader.

tribute. a forced payment of money, goods, or slaves by one nation, ruler, or group to another.

Vandal. a Germanic tribe that sacked Rome in the fifth century A.D.

vassal. a nation, group of people, or person who gives money, goods, and services to a stronger nation, group, or person in exchange for protection.

village. a small area of permanent houses and farms.

INDEX

ILLUSTRATION CREDITS: 6, British Museum • 7, (*top*) Scala; (*bottom*) Louvre, Paris • 8, photo by F.L. Kenett, © George Rainbird, Ltd. • 9, (*top*) Edward/Freelance Photographers Guild; (*bottom*) photo by F.L. Kenett, © George Rainbird Ltd., 1963 • 10, Shostal • 11, (*top*) Hurn/Magnum; (*bottom*) Kunsthistorisches Museum, Vienna, photo Meyer K.G. • 12, Louvre, Paris • 13, (*top* and *bottom*), 14, (*top*) Lessing/Magnum • 14, (*bottom*) Belzeaux/Rapho/Photo Researchers • 15, (*top*) Lessing/Magnum; (*bottom left* and *right*) Belzeaux/Rapho/Photo Reasearchers • 17, George Holton/Photo Researchers • 18, Courtesy of the Oriental Institute, University of Chicago • 21, (*top*) British Museum; (*bottom left*) British Museum, photo by Michael Holford; (*bottom right*) Scala • 25, University of Pennsylvania Library • 28, Louvre, Paris • 32, Georg Gerster/Photo Researchers • 39, 41, (*top* and *bottom*), 42, The Metropolitan Museum of Art; Gift of John D. Rockefeller, Jr. • 43, The Granger Collection • 48, Lawrence Smith/Photo Researchers • 53, Photoworld • 54, 60, The Metropolitan Museum of Art, Rogers Fund • 62, Lessing/Magnum • 64, Bildarchiv Foto Marburg/Art Resource • 66, The Metropolitan Museum of Art, photography by Egyptian Expedition • 70, Georg Gerster/Photo Researchers • 78, Hirmer Verlag/München • 84, Erich Lessing/Magnum • 86, Jewish Theological Seminary of America • 87, Shostal • 90, 91, Staatliche Museen East Berlin • 96, British Museum • 98, Courtesy of the Trustees of the British Museum • 99, British Museum, photo by Michael Holford • 100, Bettmann Archive • 104, The Metropolitan Museum of Art, The Fletcher Fund, 1956 • 107, Staatsbibliothek, Bildarchiv, West Berlin • 111, Louvre, Paris • 113, (*top*) EPA/Scala/Art Resource • 113, (*left*) Mansell Collection • 116, National Museum of Athens, photo by TAP Service; (*bottom right*) Museum of Fine Arts, Boston, H.L. Pierce Fund • 118, Museo Archeologico, Florence • 121, The Metropolitan Museum of Art, Rogers Fund, 1907 • 122, Art Resource • 130, Shostal • 133, Grunsweig/Photo Researchers • 135, The Metropolitan Museum of Art • 139, EPA/Art Resource • 141, The Granger Collection • 146, 152, Scala • 157, Art Resource • 161, Louvre, Paris, photo by Giraudon • 162, Deutsches Archeologisches Institut, West Berlin • 169, Lessing, Magnum • 172, Museum Division of Schloss Nymphenburg, Munich • 178, Leonard von Matt/Rapho/Photo Researchers • 184, Cathedral Treasury, Aachen, West Germany • 185, Art Resource • 187, The Metropolitan Museum of Art, Rogers Fund • 188, Art Resource • 193, Shostal • 198, Leonard von Matt/Art Resource • 201, Art Reference Bureau • 206, Gabinetto Fotografico Nationale, Rome.